VON CLAUSEWITZ

THE ESSENTIAL
CLAUSEWITZ

SELECTIONS FROM *ON WAR*

Carl von Clausewitz

Edited by
Joseph I. Greene

DOVER PUBLICATIONS, INC.
Mineola, New York

The woodcut portrait of Clausewitz was made
by Professor Hans A. Mueller

Bibliographical Note

This Dover edition, first published in 2003, is a republication of *The
Living Thoughts of Clausewitz*, published by Cassell and Company, Limited,
London, Toronto, Melbourne and Sydney, in 1945. We have included all of
Clausewitz's words from that edition (selected and arranged from *On War*),
but have omitted the introduction by Major-General J. F. C. Fuller.

Library of Congress Cataloging-in-Publication Data

Clausewitz, Carl von, 1780–1831.
   [Vom Kriege. English. Selections]
   The essential Clausewitz : selections from On war / Carl von
Clausewitz ; edited by Joseph I. Greene.
     p. cm.
   Originally published: The living thoughts of Clausewitz. London ;
Toronto : Cassell, 1945.
   ISBN 0-486-43083-9 (pbk.)
   1. War. 2. Military art and science. I. Greene, Joseph I. (Joseph
Ingham), b. 1897. II. Title.

U102.C63213 2003
355.02—dc21
                                     2003051279

Manufactured in the United States of America
Dover Publications, Inc., 31 East 2nd Street, Mineola, N.Y. 11501

CONTENTS

CONTENTS

IV. OFFENCE AND DEFENCE

V. PLAN OF WAR

VI. WAR AND POLITICS

VII. CONCLUSIONS

BIOGRAPHICAL NOTE

KARL VON CLAUSEWITZ was born at Burg, Prussia, June 1, 1780, and died at Breslau, in that country, November 16, 1831. Being the son of a Prussian officer militarism was, so to speak, in his veins, and he entered the army at the age of twelve. This was in 1792, and he was thus able to see two years of campaigning against the French Revolutionary armies, obtaining his commission as an officer at the age of fifteen. In 1801 he entered the War Academy in Berlin, at that time under the direction of the redoubtable Scharnhorst, and was soon his most brilliant and promising pupil. In 1803 Clausewitz became aide de camp to Prince August of Prussia, in which capacity he witnessed the rout of the Prussians at Jena, 1806, when, with his royal master, he was taken prisoner. He was confined in France until 1808. On his return to Germany Clausewitz assisted Scharnhorst in remodelling the Prussian army, but in 1812 he refused to join King Frederick William II, as an ally of Napoleon, so joined the Russian army, thus taking part, from the Russian side, in the campaign of Moscow. Rejoining his own army after that war, Clausewitz was on the staff of an army corps in the Waterloo Campaign of 1815. In the years of peace that followed he became director of the War Academy in Berlin and worked out his theory of War as embodied in the following pages. His last military activity was as chief of staff to Field Marshal Gneisenau, during the Polish insurrection of 1830.

ON THE NATURE OF WAR

THE GENIUS FOR WAR

EVERY SPECIAL CALLING IN LIFE, IF IT IS TO BE FOLLOWED WITH success, requires peculiar qualifications of understanding and soul. Where these are of a high order, and manifest themselves by extraordinary achievements, the mind to which they belong is termed *genius*.

We know very well that this word is used in many significations which are very different both in extent and nature ; but as we neither profess to be philosopher nor grammarian, we must be allowed to keep to the meaning usual in ordinary language, and to understand by " genius " a very high mental capacity for certain employments.

We wish to stop for a moment over this faculty and dignity of the mind to explain more fully the meaning of the conception. What we have to do is to bring under consideration every common tendency of the powers of the mind and soul towards the business of War, the whole of which common tendencies we may look upon as the *essence of military genius*. We say " common," for just therein consists military genius, that it is not one single quality bearing upon War, as, for instance, courage, while other qualities of mind and soul are wanting or have a direction which is unserviceable for War, but that it is *an harmonious association of powers*, in which one or other may predominate, but none must be in opposition.

The fewer the employments followed by a Nation, the more that of arms predominates, so much the more prevalent will military genius also be found. But this merely applies to its prevalence, by no means to its degree, for that depends on the general state of intellectual culture in the country. If we look at a wild, warlike race, then we find a warlike spirit in individuals much more common than in a civilized people. But amongst uncivilized people we never find a really great General, and very seldom what we can properly call a military genius, because that requires a development of the intelligent powers which cannot be found in an uncivilized state. That a civilized people may also have a warlike tendency and development is a matter of course ; and the more this is general, the more frequently also will military spirit be found in individuals in their armies. Now as this coincides in such case with the higher degree of civilization, therefore from such nations have issued forth the most brilliant military exploits, as the Romans and the French have exemplified. The greatest names in these and in all other nations that have been renowned in War belong strictly to epochs of higher culture.

From this we may infer how great a share the intelligent powers have in superior military genius. We shall now look more closely into this point.

War is the province of danger, and therefore courage above all things is the first quality of a warrior.

Courage is of two kinds : first, physical courage, or courage in presence of danger to the person ; and next, moral courage, or courage before responsibility. We only speak here of the first.

Courage before danger to the person, again, is of two kinds. First, it may be indifference to danger, whether proceeding from the organism of the individual, contempt of death, or habit : in any of these cases it is to be regarded as a permanent condition.

Secondly, courage may proceed from motives such as personal pride, patriotism, enthusiasm of any kind. In this case courage is not so much a normal condition as an impulse.

We may conceive that the two kinds act differently. The first kind is more certain, because it has become a second nature ; the second often leads him further. In the first there is more of firmness, in the second, of boldness. The first leaves the judgment cooler, the second raises its power at times, but often bewilders it. The two combined make up the most perfect kind of courage.

War is the province of physical exertion and suffering. A certain strength of body and mind is required, which produces indifference to them. With these qualifications, under the guidance of simply a sound understanding, a man is at once a proper instrument for War. If we go further in the demands which War makes on its votaries, then we find the powers of the understanding predominating. War is the province of uncertainty : three-fourths of those things upon which action in War must be calculated, are hidden more or less in the clouds of great uncertainty. Here, then, above all a fine and penetrating mind is called for.

An average intellect may, at one time, perhaps hit upon this truth by accident ; an extraordinary courage, at another, may compensate for the want of this tact ; but in the majority of cases the average result will always bring to light the deficient understanding.

War is the province of chance. In no sphere of human activity is such a margin to be left for this intruder. It increases the uncertainty of every circumstance, and deranges the course of events.

From this uncertainty of all intelligence and suppositions, the actor in War constantly finds things different from his expectations ; and this cannot fail to have an influence on his plans. If this influence is so great as to render the predetermined plan completely nugatory, then, as a rule, a new one must be substituted in its place ; but at the moment the necessary data are often wanting for this, because in the course of action circumstances press for immediate decision, and allow no time to look about for fresh data, often not enough for mature consideration.

But it more often happens that the correction of one premise, and the knowledge of chance events which have arisen, are not sufficient to overthrow our plans completely, but only suffice to produce hesitation. The reason of this is, that we do not gain all our experience at once, but by degrees ; thus our determinations continue to be assailed incessantly by fresh experience ; and the mind, if we may use the expression, must always be " under arms."

Now, if it is to get safely through this perpetual conflict with the unexpected, two qualities are indispensable : in the first place an intellect which, even in the midst of this intense obscurity, is not without some traces of inner light, and then the courage to follow this faint light. The first is figuratively expressed by the French phrase *coup d'œil*. The other is *resolution*. As the battle is the feature in War, and as time and space are important elements in it, the idea of rapid and correct decision related to the estimation of these two elements, and to denote the idea, an expression was adopted which actually only points to a correct judgment by eye. But it is undeniable that all able decisions formed in the moment of action soon came to be understood by the expression, as, for instance, the hitting upon the right point of attack, etc. It is, therefore, not only the physical, but more frequently the mental eye which is meant in *coup d'œil*. Naturally, the expression, like the thing, is always more in its place in the field of tactics : still, it must not be wanting in strategy.

Resolution is an act of courage in single instances, and if it becomes a characteristic trait, it is a habit of the mind. But here we do not mean courage in face of bodily danger, but in face of responsibility.

We have assigned to resolution the office of removing the torments of doubt, and the dangers of delay, when there are no sufficient motives for guidance. When there are *sufficient motives* in the man, let them be objective or subjective, true or false, we have no right to speak of his resolution.

This resolution now, which overcomes the state of doubting, can only be called forth by the intellect, and, in fact, by a peculiar tendency of the same. The mere union of a superior understanding and the necessary feelings are not sufficient to make up resolution. There are persons who possess the keenest perception for the most difficult problems, who are also not fearful of responsibility, and yet in cases of difficulty cannot come to a resolution. The forerunner of resolution is an act of the mind making evident the necessity of venturing. This quite peculiar direction of the mind, which conquers every other fear in man by the fear of wavering or doubting, is what makes up resolution in strong minds ; therefore, in our opinion, men who have little intelligence can never be resolute. Should our assertion appear extraordinary to any one, because he knows many a resolute officer who is no deep thinker, we must remind him that the question here is about a peculiar direction of the mind, and not about great thinking powers.

There have been many instances of men who have shown the greatest resolution in an inferior rank, and have lost it in a higher position. They see the dangers of a wrong decision, and as they are surrounded with things new to them, their understanding loses its original force, and they become only the more timid the more they become aware of the danger of the irresolution into which they have fallen.

From the *coup d'œil* and resolution we are naturally led to speak of *presence of mind*, which in War must act a great part, for it is nothing but a conquest over the unexpected. As we admire presence of mind in a pithy answer to anything said unexpectedly, so we admire it in a ready expedient on sudden danger. Neither the answer nor the expedient need be in themselves extraordinary, if they only hit the point.

Whether this noble quality of a man is to be ascribed more to his mind or to his feelings, depends on the nature of the case. A telling repartee bespeaks rather a ready wit, a ready expedient in sudden danger implies more particularly a well-balanced mind.

If we take a general view of the four elements composing the atmosphere in which War moves, of *danger, physical effort, uncertainty*, and *chance*, it is easy to conceive that a great force of mind and understanding is requisite to be able to make way with safety and success amongst such opposing elements, a force which we find termed *energy, firmness, staunchness, strength of mind and character*. All these manifestations of the heroic nature might be regarded as one and the same power of volition, modified according to circumstances; but nearly related as these things are to each other, still they are not one and the same, and it is desirable for us to distinguish here a little more closely at least the action of the powers of the soul in relation to them.

As long as his men, full of good courage, fight with zeal and spirit, it is seldom necessary for the Chief to show great energy of purpose in the pursuit of his object. But as soon as difficulties arise—and that must always happen when great results are at stake—then things no longer move on of themselves like a well-oiled machine, the machine itself then begins to offer resistance, and to overcome this the Commander must have a great force of will. By this resistance we must not exactly suppose disobedience and murmurs; it is the whole feeling of the dissolution of all physical and moral power, it is the heartrending sight of the bloody sacrifice which the Commander has to contend with in himself, and then in all others who directly or indirectly transfer to him their impressions, feelings, anxieties, and desires. Whenever his own spirit is no longer strong enough to revive the spirit of all others, the masses drawing him down with them sink into the lower region of animal nature, which shrinks from danger and knows not shame. These are the weights which the courage and intelligent faculties of the military Commander have to overcome if he is to make his name illustrious.

Energy in action expresses the strength of the motive through which the action is excited, let the motive have its origin in a conviction of the understanding, or in an impulse. But the latter can hardly ever be wanting where great force is to show itself.

Firmness denotes the resistance of the will in relation to the force of a single blow, *staunchness* in relation to a continuance of blows. Close as is the analogy between the two, and often as the one is used in place of the other, still there is a notable difference between them which cannot be mistaken, inasmuch as firmness against a single powerful impression may have its root in the mere strength of a feeling, but staunchness must be supported rather by the understanding, for the greater the duration of an action the more systematic deliberation is connected with it, and from this staunchness partly derives its power.

If we now turn to *strength of mind or soul,* then the first question is, What are we to understand thereby ?

Plainly it is not vehement expressions of feeling, nor easily excited passions, but the power of listening to reason in the midst of the most intense excitement, in the storm of the most violent passions. This counterpoise is nothing but a sense of the dignity of man, that noblest pride, that deeply-seated desire of the soul always to act as a being endowed with understanding and reason.

By the term *strength of character*, or simply *character*, is denoted tenacity of conviction ; but this kind of firmness certainly cannot manifest itself if the views themselves are subject to frequent change. Evidently we should not say of a man who changes his views every moment, however much the motives of change may originate with himself, that he has character.

Now in War, owing to the many and powerful impressions

to which the mind is exposed, and in the uncertainty of all knowledge and of all science, more things occur to distract a man from the road he has entered upon, to make him doubt himself and others, than in any other human activity.

Here often nothing will help us but an imperative maxim which, independent of reflection, at once controls it : that maxim is, in all doubtful cases to adhere to the first opinion, and not to give it up until a clear conviction forces us to do so. We must firmly believe in the superior authority of well-tried maxims, and under the dazzling influence of momentary events not forget that their value is of an inferior stamp. By this preference which in doubtful cases we give to first convictions, by adherence to the same our actions acquire that stability and consistency which make up what is called character.

Force of character leads us to a spurious variety of it— *obstinacy*.

It is often very difficult in concrete cases to say where the one ends and the other begins ; on the other hand, it does not seem difficult to determine the difference in idea.

Obstinacy is *a fault of the feelings* or heart. This inflexibility of will, this impatience of contradiction, have their origin only in a particular kind of egoism, which sets above every other pleasure that of governing both self and others by its own mind alone. We should call it a kind of vanity, were it not decidedly something better. Vanity is satisfied with mere show, but obstinacy rests upon the enjoyment of the thing.

We say, therefore, force of character degenerates into obstinacy whenever the resistance to opposing judgments proceeds not from better convictions or a reliance upon a more trustworthy maxim, but from a feeling of opposition. If this definition is of little assistance practically, still it will prevent obstinacy from being considered merely force of character intensified.

Having in these high attributes of a great military Commander made ourselves acquainted with those qualities in which heart and head co-operate, we now come to a speciality of military activity which perhaps may be looked upon as the most marked if it is not the most important, and which only makes a demand on the power of the mind, without regard to the forces of feelings. It is the connection which exists between War and country or ground.

This connection is, in the first place, a permanent condition of War, for it is impossible to imagine our organized Armies effecting any operation otherwise than in some given space ; it is, secondly, of the most decisive importance, because it modifies, at times completely alters, the action of all forces ; thirdly, while on the one hand it often concerns the most minute features of locality, on the other it may apply to immense tracts of country.

The Commander in War must commit the business he has in hand to a corresponding space which his eye cannot survey, which the keenest zeal cannot always explore, and with which, owing to the constant changes taking place, he can also seldom become properly acquainted. Certainly the enemy generally is in the same situation ; still, the difficulty, although common to both, is not the less a difficulty, and he who by talent and practice overcomes it will have a great advantage on his side.

This very peculiar difficulty must be overcome by a natural mental gift of a special kind which is known by the—too restricted—term of sense of locality (*Ortsinn*). It is the power of quickly forming a correct geometrical idea of any portion of country, and consequently of being able to find one's place in it exactly at any time. This is plainly an act of the imagination. The perception no doubt is formed partly by means of the physical eye, partly by the mind, which fills up what is wanting with ideas derived from knowledge and experience, and out of the fragments visible to the physical eye forms a whole ; but that this whole should present itself vividly to the reason, should become a picture, a mentally drawn map, that this picture should be fixed, that the details should never again separate themselves—all that can only be effected by the mental faculty which we call imagination.

It is natural that scope for the exercise of this talent should increase along with rank. If the hussar and rifleman in command of a patrol must know well all the highways and byways, and if for that a few marks, a few limited powers of observation, are sufficient, the Chief of an Army must make himself familiar with the general geographical features of a province and of a country ; must always have vividly before his eyes the direction of the roads, rivers, and hills, without at the same time being able to dispense with the narrower " sense of locality " (*Ortsinn*). No doubt, information of various kinds as to objects in general, maps, books, memoirs, and for details the assistance of his Staff, are a great help to him ; but it is nevertheless certain that if he has himself a talent for forming an ideal picture of a country quickly and distinctly, it lends to his action an easier and firmer step, saves him from a certain mental helplessness, and makes him less dependent on others.

We think we have now passed in review those manifestations of the powers of mind and soul which military activity requires from human nature. Everywhere intellect appears as an essential co-operative force ; and thus we can understand how the work of War, although so plain and simple in its effects, can never be conducted with distinguished success by people without distinguished powers of the understanding.

OF DANGER AND BODILY EXERTION IN WAR

USUALLY before we have learnt what danger really is, we form an idea of it which is rather attractive than repulsive. In the intoxication of enthusiasm, to fall upon the enemy at the charge —who cares then about bullets and men falling ? To throw oneself, blinded by excitement for a moment, against cold death, uncertain whether we or another shall escape him, and all this close to the golden gate of victory, close to the rich fruit which ambition thirsts for—can this be difficult ? It will not be difficult, and still less will it appear so. But such moments, which, however, are not the work of a single pulse-beat, as is supposed, but rather like doctors' draughts, must be taken diluted and spoilt by mixture with time—such moments, we say, are but few.

The young soldier cannot reach any of the different strata of danger without feeling that the light of reason does not move here in the same medium, that it is not refracted in the same manner as in speculative contemplation. Indeed, he must be a very extraordinary man who, under these impressions for the first time, does not lose the power of making any instantaneous decisions. It is true that habit soon blunts such impressions ; in half an hour we begin to be more or less indifferent to all that is going on around us : but an ordinary character never

attains to complete coolness and the natural elasticity of mind ;
and so we perceive that here again ordinary qualities will not
suffice—a thing which gains truth, the wider the sphere of
activity which is to be filled. Enthusiastic, stoical, natural
bravery, great ambition, or also long familiarity with danger—
much of all this there must be if all the effects produced in this
resistant medium are not to fall far short of that which in the
student's chamber may appear only the ordinary standard.

Amongst the many things in War for which no tariff can be
fixed, bodily effort may be specially reckoned. Provided there
is no waste, it is a coefficient of all the forces, and no one can
tell exactly to what extent it may be carried. But what is
remarkable is, that just as only a strong arm enables the archer
to stretch the bowstring to the utmost extent, so also in War
it is only by means of a great directing spirit that we can expect
the full power latent in the troops to be developed. For it is
one thing if an Army, in consequence of great misfortunes,
surrounded with danger, falls all to pieces like a wall that has
been thrown down, and can only find safety in the utmost
exertion of its bodily strength ; it is another thing entirely
when a victorious Army, drawn on by proud feelings only,
is conducted at the will of its Chief. The same effort which in
the one case might at most excite our pity must in the other call
forth our admiration, because it is much more difficult to sustain.

We have spoken here of bodily effort, chiefly because, like
danger, it belongs to the fundamental causes of friction, and
because its indefinite quantity makes it like an elastic body, the
friction of which is well known to be difficult to calculate.

To check the abuse of these considerations, of such a survey
of things which aggravate the difficulties of War, nature has
given our judgment a guide in our sensibilities. Just as an
individual cannot with advantage refer to his personal deficiences
if he is insulted and ill-treated, but may well do so if he has
successfully repelled the affront, or has fully revenged it, so no
Commander or Army will lessen the impression of a disgraceful
defeat by depicting the danger, the distress, the exertions, things
which would immensely enhance the glory of a victory. Thus
our feeling, which after all is only a higher kind of judgment,
forbids us to do what seems an act of justice to which our
judgment would be inclined.

INFORMATION IN WAR

By the word " information " we denote all the knowledge which we have of the enemy and his country ; therefore, in fact, the foundation of all our ideas and actions. Let us just consider the nature of this foundation, its want of trustworthiness, its changefulness, and we shall soon feel what a dangerous edifice War is, how easily it may fall to pieces and bury us in its ruins.

Great part of the information obtained in War is contradictory, a still greater part is false, and by far the greatest part is of a doubtful character. What is required of an officer is a certain power of discrimination, which only knowledge of men and things and good judgment can give. The law of probability must be his guide. This is not a trifling difficulty even in respect of the first plans, which can be formed in the chamber outside the real sphere of War, but it is enormously increased when in the thick of War itself one report follows hard upon the heels of another ; it is then fortunate if these reports in contradicting each other show a certain balance of probability, and thus themselves call forth a scrutiny. It is much worse for the unexperienced when accident does not render him this service, but one report supports another, confirms it, magnifies it, finishes off the picture with fresh touches of colour, until necessity in urgent haste forces from us a resolution which will soon be discovered to be folly, all these reports having been lies, exaggerations, errors, etc.

As a general rule, every one is more inclined to lend credence to the bad than to the good. Every one is inclined to magnify the bad in some measure. Firm in reliance on his own better convictions, the Chief must stand like a rock against which the sea breaks its fury in vain. The *rôle* is not easy. The impression of the senses is stronger than the force of the ideas resulting from methodical reflection, and this goes so far that no important undertaking was ever yet carried out without the Commander having to subdue new doubts in himself at the time of commencing the execution of his work. Firm reliance on self must make him proof against the seeming pressure of the moment ; his first conviction will in the end prove true, when the foreground scenery which fate has pushed on to the stage of War, with its accompaniments of terrific objects, is drawn aside and the horizon extended. This is one of the great chasms which separate *conception* from *execution*.

FRICTION IN WAR

As long as we have no personal knowledge of War, we cannot conceive where those difficulties lie of which so much is said, and what that genius and those extraordinary mental powers required in a General have really to do. All appears so simple, all the requisite branches of knowledge appear so plain, all the combinations so unimportant, that in comparison with them the easiest problem in higher mathematics impresses us with a certain scientific dignity. But if we have seen War, all becomes intelligible.

Everything is very simple in War, but the simplest thing is difficult. These difficulties accumulate and produce a friction which no man can imagine exactly who has not seen War. Suppose now a traveller, who towards evening expects to accomplish the two stages at the end of his day's journey, four or five leagues, with post-horses, on the high road—it is nothing. He arrives now at the last station but one, finds no horses, or very bad ones ; then a hilly country, bad roads ; it is a dark night, and he is glad when, after a great deal of trouble, he reaches the next station, and finds there some miserable accommodation. So in War, through the influence of an infinity of petty circumstances, which cannot properly be described on paper, things disappoint us, and we fall short of the mark. A powerful iron will overcomes this friction ; it crushes the obstacles, but certainly the machine along with them.

Friction is the only conception which in a general way corresponds to that which distinguishes real War from War on paper. The military machine, the Army and all belonging to it, is in fact simple, and appears on this account easy to manage. But let us reflect that no part of it is in one piece, that it is composed entirely of individuals, each of which keeps up its own friction in all directions. The danger which War brings with it, the bodily exertions which it requires, augment this evil so much that they may be regarded as the greatest causes of it.

This enormous friction is therefore everywhere brought

into contact with chance, and thus incidents take place upon which it was impossible to calculate. As an instance of one such chance take the weather. Here the fog prevents the enemy from being discovered in time, a battery from firing at the right moment, a report from reaching the General ; there the rain prevents a battalion from arriving at the right time, because instead of for three it had to march perhaps eight hours ; it prevents the cavalry from charging effectively because it is stuck fast in heavy ground.

Activity in War is movement in a resistant medium. Just as a man immersed in water is unable to perform with ease and regularity the most natural and simplest movement, that of walking, so in War, with ordinary powers, one cannot keep even the line of mediocrity.

The knowledge of this friction is a chief part of that experience in War, so often talked of, which is required in a good General. Certainly he is not the best General in whose mind it assumes the greatest dimensions, who is the most over-awed by it ; but a General must be aware of it that he may overcome it, where that is possible, and that he may not expect a degree of precision in results which is impossible on account of this very friction.

Now is there, then, no kind of oil capable of diminishing this friction ? Only one, and that one is not always available at the will of the Commander or his Army. It is the habituation of an Army to War.

Habit gives strength to the body in great exertion, to the mind in great danger, to the judgment against first impressions.

As the human eye in a dark room dilates its pupil, draws in the little light that there is, partially distinguishes objects by degrees, and at last knows them quite well, so it is in War with the experienced soldier, whilst the novice is only met by pitch dark night.

Habituation to War no General can give his Army at once, and manœuvres (peace exercises) furnish but a weak substitute for it, weak in comparison with real experience in War, but not weak in relation to other Armies in which the training is limited to mere mechanical exercises of routine. So to regulate the exercises in peace time as to include some of these causes of friction, that the judgment, circumspection, even resolution of the separate leaders may be brought into exercise, is of much greater consequence than those believe who do not know the thing by experience. It is of immense importance that the soldier, high or low, whatever rank he has, should not have to encounter in War those things which, when seen for the first time, set him in astonishment and perplexity ; if he has only met with them one single time before, even by that he is half acquainted with them. This relates even to bodily fatigues. They should be practised less to accustom the body to them than the mind. In War the young soldier is very apt to regard unusual fatigues as the consequence of faults, mistakes, and embarrassment in the conduct of the whole, and to become distressed and despondent as a consequence. This would not happen if he had been prepared for this beforehand by exercises in peace.

A State which has been long at peace should, therefore, always seek to procure some officers who have done good service at the different scenes of Warfare, or to send there some of its own, that they may get a lesson in War.

II

ON THE THEORY OF WAR

BRANCHES OF THE ART OF WAR

WAR IN ITS LITERAL MEANING IS FIGHTING, FOR FIGHTING ALONE is the efficient principle in the manifold activity which in a wide sense is called War. But fighting is a trial of strength of the moral and physical forces by means of the latter. That the moral cannot be omitted is evident of itself, for the condition of the mind has always the most decisive influence on the forces employed in War.

The necessity of fighting very soon led men to special inventions to turn the advantage in it in their own favour : in consequence of these the mode of fighting has undergone great alterations ; but in whatever way it is conducted its conception remains unaltered, and fighting is that which constitutes War.

Fighting has determined everything appertaining to arms and equipment, and these in turn modify the mode of fighting ; there is, therefore, a reciprocity of action between the two.

The Art of War is therefore, in its proper sense, the art of making use of the given means in fighting, and we cannot give it a better name than the " *Conduct of War*." On the other hand, in a wider sense all activities which have their existence on account of War, therefore the whole creation of troops, that is levying them, arming, equipping, and exercising them, belong to the Art of War.

The conduct of War is the formation and conduct of the fighting. If this fighting was a single act, there would be no necessity for any further subdivision, but the fight is composed of a greater or less number of single acts, complete in themselves, which we call combats, and which form new units. From this arises the totally different activities, that of the *formation* and *conduct* of these single combats in themselves, and the *combination* of them with one another, with a view to the ultimate object of the War. The first is called *tactics*, the other *strategy*.

Tactics is the theory of the use of military forces in combat. Strategy *is the theory of the use of combats for the object of the War.*

Our classification reaches and covers only the *use of the military force.* But now there are in War a number of activities which are subservient to it, and still are quite different from it ; sometimes closely allied, sometimes less near in their affinity. All these activities relate to the *maintenance of the military force.* But, strictly viewed, all activities thus connected with it are always to be regarded only as preparations for fighting. We have therefore a right to exclude them from the Art of War in its restricted sense, from the conduct of War properly so called ; and we are obliged to do so if we would comply with the first principle of all theory, the elimination of all heterogeneous elements. Who would include in the real " conduct of War " the whole litany of subsistence and administration, because it is admitted to stand in constant reciprocal action with the use of the troops, but is something essentially different from it ?

The subjects which constitute the activities outside of the combat are of various kinds. The subjects which belong to the fighting itself are *marches, camps,* and *cantonments.*

The other subjects, which only belong to the maintenance, are *subsistance, care of the sick, the supply and repair of arms and equipment.*

Marches are quite identical with the use of the troops. The act of marching in the *combat,* generally called manœuvring, certainly does not necessarily include the use of weapons, but it is so completely and necessarily combined with it that it forms an integral part of that which we call a combat. But the march outside the combat is nothing but the execution of a strategic measure. By the strategic plan is settled *when, where, and with what forces* a battle is to be delivered—and to carry that into execution the march is the only means.

The march outside of the combat is therefore an instrument of strategy, but not on that account exclusively a subject of strategy. If we prescribe to a column its route on a particular side of a river or of a branch of a mountain, then that is a strategic measure, for it contains the intention of fighting on that particular side of the hill or river in preference to the other, in case a combat should be necessary during the march.

But if a column, instead of following the road through a

valley, marches along the parallel ridge of heights, or for the convenience of marching divides itself into several columns, then these are tactical arrangements, for they relate to the manner in which we shall use the troops in the anticipated combat.

Camps, by which we mean every disposition of troops in concentrated, therefore in battle order, in contradistinction to cantonments or quarters, are a state of rest, therefore of restoration ; but they are at the same time also the strategic appointment of a battle on the spot chosen ; and by the manner in which they are taken up they contain the fundamental lines or the battle, a condition from which every defensive battle starts ; they are therefore essential parts of both strategy and tactics.

Cantonments take the place of camps for the better refreshment of the troops. They are therefore, like camps, strategic subjects as regards position and extent ; tactical subjects as regards internal organization, with a view to readiness to fight.

The occupation of camps and cantonments no doubt usually combines with the recuperation of the troops another object also, for example, the covering a district of country, the holding a position ; but it can very well be only the first. We remind our readers that strategy may follow a great diversity of objects, for everything which appears an advantage may be the object of a combat, and the preservation of the instrument with which War is made must necessarily very often become the object of its partial combinations.

But if the maintenance of the troops in camp or quarters calls forth activities which are no employment of the armed force, such as the construction of huts, pitching of tents, subsistence and sanitary services in camps or quarters, then such belong neither to strategy nor tactics.

Amongst the subjects which belong to the mere keeping up of an armed force, because none of the parts are identified with the combat, the victualling of the troops themselves come first, as it must be done almost daily and for each individual. Thus it is that it completely permeates military action in the parts constituting strategy—we say parts constituting strategy, because during a battle the subsistence of troops will rarely have any influence in modifying the plan, although the thing is conceivable enough. There is nothing more common than for the leading strategic features of a campaign and War to be traced out in connection with a view to this supply.

The other branches of administrative activity which we have mentioned stand much farther apart from the use of the troops. The *care of sick and wounded*, highly important as it is for the good of an Army, directly affects it only in a small portion of the individuals composing it, and therefore has only a weak and indirect influence upon the use of the rest. The *completing and replacing articles of arms and equipment*, except so far as by the organism of the forces it constitutes a continuous activity inherent in them—takes place only periodically, and therefore seldom affects strategic plans.

We must, however, here guard ourselves against a mistake. In certain cases these subjects may be really of decisive importance. The distance of hospitals and depots of munitions may very easily be imagined as the sole cause of very important strategic decisions. But we are at present occupied not with the particular facts of a concrete case, but with abstract theory.

If we have clearly understood the results of our reflections, then the activities belonging to War divide themselves into two principal classes, into such as are only " *preparations for War* " and into the " *War itself*." This division must therefore also be made in theory.

The present theory will treat the combat as the real contest, marches, camps, and cantonments as circumstances which are more or less identical with it. The subsistence of the troops will only come into consideration like *other given circumstances* in respect of its results, not as an activity belonging to the combat.

The Art of War thus viewed in its limited sense divides itself again into tactics and strategy. The former occupies itself with the form of the separate combat, the latter with its use. Both connect themselves with the circumstances of marches, camps, cantonments only through the combat, and these circumstances are tactical or strategic according as they relate to the form or to the signification of the battle.

No doubt there will be many readers who will consider superfluous this careful separation of two things lying so close together as tactics and strategy, because it has no direct effect on the conduct itself of War. We admit, certainly that it would be pedantry to look for direct effects on the field of battle from a theoretical distinction.

But the first business of every theory is to clear up conceptions and ideas which have been jumbled together, and, we may say, entangled and confused ; and only when a right understanding is established, as to names and conceptions, can we hope to progress with clearness and facility.

ON THE THEORY OF WAR

Formerly by the term " Art of War," or " Science of War," nothing was understood but the totality of those branches of knowledge and those appliances of skill occupied with material things.

In the art of sieges we first perceive a certain degree of guidance of the combat, something of the action of the intellectual faculties upon the material forces placed under their control, but generally only so far that it very soon embodied itself again in new material forms, such as approaches, trenches, counter-approaches, batteries, etc.

Afterwards tactics attempted to give to the mechanism of its joints the character of a general disposition, built upon the peculiar properties of the instrument, which character leads indeed to the battle-field, but instead of leading to the free activity of mind, leads to an Army made like an automaton.

The conduct of War properly so called, that is, a use of the prepared means adapted to the most special requirements, was not considered as any suitable subject for theory, but one which should be left to natural talents alone.

As contemplation on War continually increased, and its history every day assumed more of a critical character, the urgent want appeared of the support of fixed maxims and rules, in order that in the controversies naturally arising about military events the war of opinions might be brought to some one point.

The superiority in numbers was chosen from amongst all the factors required to produce victory, because it could be brought under mathematical laws through combinations of time and space. This would have been very well if it had been done to gain a preliminary knowledge of this one factor, according to its relations, but to make it a rule for ever to consider superiority of numbers as the sole law ; to see the whole secret of the Art of War in the formula, *in a certain time, at a certain point, to bring up superior masses*—was a restriction overruled by the force of realities.

An ingenious author tried to concentrate in a single conception, that of a *Base*, a whole host of objects. The list comprised the subsistence of the troops, the keeping them complete in numbers and equipment, the security of communications with the home country, lastly, the security of retreat in case it became necessary ; and, first of all, he proposed to substitute this conception of a base for all these things ; then for the base itself to substitute its own length (extent) ; and, last of all, to substitute the angle formed by the army with this base : all this was done merely to obtain a pure geometrical result utterly useless.

The idea of a base is a real necessity for strategy ; but to make such a use of it as we have depicted is completely inadmissible, and could not but lead to partial conclusions which have forced these theorists into a direction opposed to common sense, namely, to a belief in the decisive effect of the enveloping form of attack.

As a reaction against this false direction, another geometrical principle, that of the so-called interior lines, was then elevated to the throne. Although this principle rests on a sound foundation, on the truth that the combat is the only effectual means in War, still it is, just on account of its purely geometrical nature, nothing but another case of one-sided theory.

All these attempts at theory are only to be considered in their analytical part as progress in the province of truth, but in their synthetical part, in their precepts and rules, they are quite unserviceable.

They strive after determinate quantities, whilst in War all is undetermined, and the calculation has always to be made with varying quantities.

They direct the attention only upon material forces, while the whole military action is penetrated throughout by intelligent forces and their effects.

They only pay regard to activity on one side, whilst War is a constant state of reciprocal action, the effects of which are mutual.

All that was not attainable by such miserable philosophy, the offspring of partial views, lay outside the precincts of science—and was the field of genius, which *raises itself above rules*.

Pity the warrior who is contented to crawl about in this beggardom of rules !

Pity the theory which sets itself in opposition to the mind ! It cannot repair this contradiction by any humility, and the humbler it is so much the sooner will ridicule and contempt drive it our of real life.

MORAL QUANTITIES IN WAR

The activity in War is never directed solely against matter ; it is always at the same time directed against the intelligent force which gives life to this matter, and to separate the two from each other is impossible.

Every one knows the moral effect of a surprise, of an attack in flank or rear. Every one thinks less of the enemy's courage as soon as he turns his back, and ventures much more in pursuit than when pursued. Every one judges of the enemy's General by his reputed talents, by his age and experience, and shapes his course accordingly. Every one casts a scrutinizing glance at the spirit and feeling of his own and the enemy's troops. All these and similar effects in the province of the moral nature of man have established themselves by experience, are perpetually recurring, and therefore warrant our reckoning them as real quantities of their kind. What could we do with any theory which should leave them out of consideration ?

In order to comprehend clearly the difficulty of the proposition which is contained in a theory for the conduct of War, we must take a closer view of the chief particulars which make up the nature of activity in War.

The first of these specialities consists in the moral forces and effects.

The combat is, in its origin, the expression of *hostile feeling*, but in our great combats, which we call Wars, the hostile feeling frequently resolves itself into merely a hostile *view*, and there is usually no innate hostile feeling residing in individual against individual. Nevertheless, the combat never passes off without such feelings being brought into activity ; for an act of violence which any one commits upon us by order of his superior, will excite in us a desire to retaliate and be revenged on him, sooner than on the superior power at whose command the act was done. This is human, or animal if we will ; still it is so.

Besides that excitation of feelings naturally arising from the combat itself, there are others also which do not essentially belong to it, but which, on account of their relationship, easily unite with it—ambition, love of power, enthusiasm of every kind, etc., etc.

Finally, the combat begets the element of danger, in which all the activities of War must live and move, like the bird in the air or the fish in the water. But the influences of danger all pass into the feelings, either directly—that is, instinctively—or through the medium of the understanding. The effect in the first case would be a desire to escape from the danger, and, if that cannot be done, fright and anxiety. If this effect does not take place, then it is *courage*, which is a counterpoise to that instinct. Courage is, however, by no means an act of the understanding, but likewise a feeling, like fear ; the latter looks to the physical preservation, courage to the moral preservation. Courage, then, is a nobler instinct. But because it is so, it will not allow itself to be used as a lifeless instrument, which produces its effects exactly according to prescribed measure. Courage is therefore no mere counterpoise to danger in order to neutralize the latter in its effects, but a peculiar power in itself.

But to estimate exactly the influence of danger upon the principal actors in War, we must not limit its sphere to the physical danger of the moment. It dominates over the actor, not only by threatening him, but also by threatening all entrusted to him, not only at the moment in which it is actually present, but also through the imagination at all other moments, which have a connection with the present ; lastly, not only directly by itself, but also indirectly by the responsibility which makes it bear with tenfold weight on the mind of the chief actor. Who could advise, or resolve upon a great battle, without feeling his mind more or less wrought up, or perplexed by, the danger and responsibility which such a great act of decision carries in itself ? We may say that action in War, in so far as it is real action, not a mere condition, is never out of the sphere of danger.

If we look upon these affections which are excited by hostility and danger as peculiarly belonging to War, we do not, therefore, exclude from it all others accompanying man in his life's journey. Certainly we may say that many a petty action of the passions is silenced in this serious business of life ; but that holds good only in respect to those acting in a lower sphere.

In higher regions it is otherwise, for the higher a man's rank, the more he must look around him ; then arise interests on every side, and a manifold activity of the passions of good and bad. Envy and generosity, pride and humility, fierceness and tenderness, all may appear as active powers in this great drama.

The second peculiarity in War is the living reaction, and the reciprocal action resulting therefrom. The effect which any measure produces upon the enemy is the most distinct of all the data which action affords ; but every theory must keep to classes (or groups) of phenomena, and can never take up the really individual case in itself. It is therefore natural that in a business such as War, which in its plan—built upon general circumstances—is so often thwarted by unexpected and singular accidents, more must generally be left to talent ; and less use can be made of a *theoretical guide* than in any other.

Lastly, the great uncertainty of all data in War is a peculiar difficulty, because all action must, to a certain extent, be planned in a mere twilight, which gives to things exaggerated dimensions and an unnatural appearance.

With materials of this kind we can only say to ourselves that it is a sheer impossibility to construct for the Art of War a theory which, like a scaffolding, shall ensure to the chief actor an external support on all sides. In all those cases in which he is thrown upon his talent he would find himself away from this scaffolding of theory, and the same result would ensue of which we spoke when we said that talent and genius act beyond the law, and theory is in opposition to reality.

Two means present themselves of getting out of this difficulty. In the first place, what we have said of the nature of military action in general does not apply in the same manner to the action of every one, whatever may be his standing.

Further, according to a division of the subject in *agreement with its nature*, the difficulties are not everywhere the same, but diminish the more results manifest themselves in the material world, and increase the more they pass into the moral. Therefore it is easier to determine, by theoretical rules, the order and conduct of a battle, than the use to be made of the battle itself. In a word, it is easier to make a theory for *tactics* than for *strategy*.

The second opening for the possibility of a theory lies in the point of view that it does not necessarily require to be a *direction* for action. As a general rule, whenever an *activity* is for the most part occupied with the same objects over and over again, with the same ends and means, such things are capable of becoming a subject of study for the reasoning faculties. But such study is just the most essential part of every *theory*, and has a peculiar title to that name.

If theory investigates the subjects which constitute War ; if it separates more distinctly that which at first sight seems amalgamated ; if it shows their probable effects ; if it makes evident the nature of objects ; if it brings to bear all over the field of War the light of essentially critical investigation—then it has fulfilled the chief duties of its province. It becomes then a guide to him who wishes to make himself acquainted with War from books ; it lights up the whole road for him, facilitates his progress, educates his judgment, and shields him from error.

III

OF STRATEGY IN GENERAL

STRATEGY

STRATEGY IS THE EMPLOYMENT OF THE BATTLE TO GAIN THE end of the War ; it must therefore give an aim to the whole military action, which must be in accordance with the object of the War ; in other words, Strategy forms the plan of the War, and to this end it links together the series of acts which are to lead to the final decision, that is to say, it makes the plans for the separate campaigns and regulates the combats to be fought in each. As these are all things which to a great extent can only be determined on conjectures some of which turn out incorrect, while a number of other arrangements pertaining to details cannot be made at all beforehand, it follows, as a matter of course, that Strategy must go with the Army to the field in order to arrange particulars on the spot, and to make the modifications in the general plan which incessantly become necessary in War. Strategy can therefore never take its hand from the work for a moment.

That this, however, has not always been the view taken is evident from the former custom of keeping Strategy in the cabinet and not with the Army, a thing only allowable if the cabinet is so near to the Army that it can be taken for the chief headquarters of the Army.

Theory will therefore attend on Strategy in the determination of its plans, or, as we may more properly say, it will throw a light on things in themselves, and on their relations to each other, and bring out prominently the little that there is of principle or rule.

If we recall how many things of the highest importance War touches upon, we may conceive that a consideration of all requires a rare grasp of mind.

A Prince or General who knows exactly how to organize his War according to his object and means, who does neither too little nor too much, gives by that the greatest proof of his genius. But the effects of this talent are exhibited not so much by the invention of new modes of action, which might strike the eye immediately, as in the successful final result of the whole. It is the exact fulfilment of silent suppositions, it is the noiseless harmony of the whole action which we should admire, and which only makes itself known in the total result.

The inquirer who, tracing back from the final result, does not perceive the signs of that harmony is one who is apt to seek for genius where it is not, and where it cannot be found.

The means and forms which Strategy uses are in fact so extremely simple, so well known by their constant repetition, that it only appears ridiculous to sound common sense when it hears critics so frequently speaking of them with high-flown emphasis. Turning a flank, which has been done a thousand times, is regarded here as a proof of the most brilliant genius, there as a proof of the most profound penetration, indeed even of the most comprehensive knowledge.

Let us admit: there is no question here about scientific formulas and problems; the relations of material things are all very simple; the right comprehension of the moral forces which come into play is more difficult. Still, even in respect to them, it is only in the highest branches of Strategy that moral complications and a great diversity of quantities and relations are to be looked for, only at that point where Strategy borders on political science, or rather where the two become one, and there, as we have before observed, they have more influence on the " how much " and " how little " is to be done than on the form of execution. Where the latter is the principal question, as in the single acts both great and small in War, the moral quantities are already reduced to a very small number.

Thus, then, in Strategy everything is very simple, but not on that account very easy. Once it is determined from the relations of the State what should and may be done by War, then the way to it is easy to find; but to follow that way straightforward, to carry out the plan without being obliged to deviate from it a thousand times by a thousand varying influences, requires, besides great strength of character, great clearness and steadiness of mind, and out of a thousand men who are remarkable, some for mind, others for penetration, others again for boldness or strength of will, perhaps not one will combine in himself all those qualities which are required to raise a man above mediocrity in the career of a general.

It may sound strange, but for all who know War in this respect it is a fact beyond doubt, that much more strength of will is required to make an important decision in Strategy than in tactics. In the latter we are hurried on with the moment; a Commander feels himself borne along in a strong current, against which he durst not contend without the most destructive consequences, he suppresses the rising fears, and boldly ventures further. In Strategy, where all goes on at a slower rate, there is more room allowed for our own apprehensions and those of others, for objections and remonstrances, consequently also for unseasonable regrets; and as we do not see things in Strategy as we do at least half of them in tactics, with the living eye, but everything must be conjectured and assumed, the convictions produced are less powerful. The consequence is that most Generals, when they should act, remain stuck fast in bewildering doubts.

Now let us cast a glance at history—upon Frederick the Great's campaign of 1760, celebrated for its fine marches and manœuvres: a perfect masterpiece of Strategic skill as critics tell us. Is there really anything to drive us out of our wits with admiration in the King's first trying to turn Daun's right flank, then his left, then again his right, etc.? Are we to see profound wisdom in this? No, that we cannot, if we are to decide naturally and without affectation. What we rather admire above all is the sagacity of the King in this respect, that while pursuing a great object with very limited means, he undertook nothing beyond his powers, and *just enough* to gain his object.

To bring Silesia into the safe harbour of a well-guaranteed peace was his object.

At the head of a small State, which was like other States in most things, and only ahead of them in some branches of administration; he could not be an Alexander, and, had he been a Charles XII,[1] he would only, like him, have broken his head. We find, therefore, in the whole of his conduct of War, a controlled power, always well balanced, and never wanting in energy, which in the most critical moments rises to astonishing

---

[1] King of Sweden (1682–1718) a great conqueror in his time.—Ed.

deeds, and the next moment oscillates quietly on again in sub-ordination to the play of the most subtle political influences. Neither vanity, thirst for glory, nor vengeance could make him deviate from his course, and this course alone it is which brought him to a fortunate termination of the contest.

Is it to be supposed that all Frederick the Great's tactical manœuvres could have been done without producing great friction in the machine ? Can the mind of a Commander elaborate such movements with the same ease as the hand of a land surveyor using the astrolabe ? Does not the sight of the sufferings of their hungry, thirsty comrades pierce the hearts of the Commander and his Generals a thousand times ? Must not the murmurs and doubts which these cause reach his ear ? Has an ordinary man the courage to demand such sacrifices, and would not such efforts most certainly demoralize the Army, break up the bands of discipline, and, in short, undermine its military virtue, if firm reliance on the greatness and infallibility of the Commander did not compensate for all ? Here, therefore, it is that we should pay respect ; it is these miracles of execution which we should admire. But it is impossible to realize all this in its full force without a foretaste of it by experience. He who only knows War from books or the drill-ground cannot realize the whole effect of this counterpoise in action ; *we beg him, therefore, to accept from us on faith and trust all that he is unable to supply from any personal experiences of his own.*

MORAL FORCES AND MILITARY VIRTUES

Moral forces form the spirit which permeates the whole being of War. They fasten themselves soonest and with the greatest affinity on to the Will which puts in motion and guides the whole mass of powers, uniting with it as it were in one stream because this is a moral force itself.

The spirit and other moral qualities which animate an Army, a General, or Governments, public opinion in provinces in which a War is raging, the moral effect of a victory or of a defeat, are things which in themselves vary very much in their nature, and which also, according as they stand with regard to our object and our relations, may have an influence in different ways.

Although little or nothing can be said about these things in books, still they belong to the theory of the Art of War, as much as everything else which constitutes War. In every rule relating to the physical forces, theory must present to the mind at the same time the share which the moral powers will have in it, if it would not be led to categorical propositions, at one time too timid and contracted, at another too dogmatical and wide. Even the most matter-of-fact theories have, without knowing it, strayed over into this moral kingdom ; for, as an example, the effects of a victory cannot in any way be explained without taking into consideration the moral impressions. And therefore the most of the subjects which we shall go through in this book are composed half of physical, half of moral causes and effects, and we might say the physical are almost no more than the wooden handle, whilst the moral are the noble metal, the real bright-polished weapon.

The value of the moral powers, and their frequently incredible influence, are best exemplified by history, and this is the most generous and the purest nourishment which the mind of the General can extract from it.—At the same time it is to be observed, that it is less demonstrations, critical examinations, and learned treatises, than sentiments, general impressions, and single flashing sparks of truth, which yield the seeds of knowledge that are no fertilise the mind.

The chief moral powers are *The Talents of the Commander ; The Military Virtue of the Army ; Its National Feeling.* Which of these is the most important no one can tell in a general way, for it is very difficult to say anything in general of their strength, and still more difficult to compare the strength of one with that of another. The best plan is not to undervalue any of them.

It is true, however, that in modern times the Armies have arrived very much at a par as regards discipline and fitness for service, and that the conduct of War has—as philosophers would say—naturally developed itself, thereby become a method, common as it were to all Armies, so that even from Commanders there is nothing further to be expected in the way of application of special means of Art, in the limited sense. Hence it cannot be denied that, as matters now stand, greater scope is afforded for the influence of National spirit and habituation of an army to War.

The national spirit of an Army (enthusiasm, fanatical zeal, faith, opinion) displays itself most in mountain warfare, where every one down to the common soldier is left to himself. On this account, a mountainous country is the best campaigning ground for popular levies.

Expertness of an Army through training, and that well-tempered courage which holds the ranks together as if they had been cast in a mould, show their superiority in an open country.

The talent of a General has most room to display itself in a closely intersected, undulating country. In mountains he has too little command over the separate parts, and the direction of all is beyond his powers ; in open plains it is simple and does not exceed those powers.

According to these undeniable elective affinities, plans should be regulated.

Military virtue of an army is distinguished from mere bravery, and still more from enthusiasm for the business of War. The first is certainly a necessary constituent part of it, but in the same way as bravery, which is a natural gift in some men, may arise in a soldier as a part of an Army from habit and custom, so with him it must also have a different direction from that which it has with others. It must lose that impulse to unbridled activity and exercise of force which is its characteristic in the individual, and submit itself to demands of a higher kind, to obedience, order, rule, and method. Enthusiasm for the profession gives life and greater fire to the military virtue of an Army, but does not necessarily constitute a part of it.

War is a special business, and however general its relations may be, and even if all the male population of a country, capable of bearing arms, exercise this calling, still it always continues to be different and separate from the other pursuits which occupy the life of man. To be imbued with a sense of the spirit and nature of this business, to make use of, to rouse, to assimilate into the system the powers which should be active in it, to penetrate completely into the nature of the business with the understanding, through exercise to gain confidence and expertness in it, to be completely given up to it, to pass out of the man into the part which it is assigned to us to play in War, that is the *military virtue of an Army* in the individual.

However much pains may be taken to combine the soldier and the citizen in one and the same individual, whatever may be done to nationalize Wars, and however much we may imagine times have changed since the days of the old Condottieri, never will it be possible to do away with the individuality of the business ; and if that cannot be done, then those who belong to it, as long as they belong to it, will always look upon themselves as a kind of guild, in the regulations, laws and customs in which the " Spirit of War " by preference finds its expression. And so it is in fact. Even with the most decided inclination to look at War from the highest point of view, it would be very wrong to look down upon this corporate spirit (*ésprit de corps*) which may and should exist more or less in every Army. This corporate spirit forms the bond of union between the natural forces which are active in that which we have called military virtue. The crystals of military virtue have a greater affinity for the spirit of a corporate body than for anything else.

An Army which preserves its usual formations under the heaviest fire, which is never shaken by imaginary fears, and in the face of real danger disputes the ground inch by inch, which, proud in the feeling of its victories, never loses its sense of obedience, its respect for and confidence in its leaders, even under the depressing effects of defeat ; an Army with all its physical powers, inured to privations and fatigue by exercise, like the muscles of an athlete ; an Army which looks upon all its toils as the means to victory, not as a curse which hovers over its standards, and which is always reminded of its duties and virtues by the short catechism of one idea, namely the *honour of its arms* ; such an Army is imbued with the true military spirit.

Soldiers may fight bravely like the Vendéans, and do great things like the Swiss, the Americans, or Spaniards, without displaying this military virtue. A Commander may also be successful at the head of standing Armies, like Eugene and Marlborough, without enjoying the benefit of its assistance ; we must not, therefore, say that a successful War without it cannot be imagined ; and we draw especial attention to that point, in order the more to individualize the conception which is here brought forward, that the idea may not dissolve into a generalization, and that it may not be thought that military

virtue is in the end everything. It is not so. Military virtue
in an Amy is a definite moral power which may be supposed
wanting, and the influence of which may therefore be estimated
—like any instrument the power of which may be calculated.

Having thus characterized it, we proceed to consider what
can be predicated of its influence, and what are the means of
gaining its assistance.

Military virtue is for the parts, what the genius of the Commander is for the whole. The General can only guide the whole,
not each separate part, and where he cannot guide the part,
there military virtue must be its leader. A General is chosen
by the reputation of his superior talents, the chief leaders of
large masses after careful probation ; but this probation dimishes
as we descend the scale of rank, and in just the same measure
we may reckon less and less upon individual talents ; but what
is wanting in this respect military virtue should supply. The
natural qualities of a war-like people play just this part : bravery
aptitude, powers of endurance and *enthusiasm.*

These properties may therefore supply the place of military
virtue, and *vice versa,* from which the following may be
deduced :

1. Military virtue is a quality of standing Armies only, but
they require it the most. In national risings its place is supplied
by natural qualities, which develop themselves there more
rapidly.

2. Standing Armies opposed to standing Armies, can more
easily dispense with it, than a standing Army opposed to a
national insurrection, for in that case, the troops are more
scattered, and the divisions left more to themselves. But
where an Army can be kept concentrated, the genius of the
General takes a greater place, and supplies what is wanting in
the spirit of the Army. Therefore generally military virtue
becomes more necessary the more the theatre of operations and
other circumstances make the War complicated, and cause
the forces to be scattered.

From these truths the only lesson to be derived is this, that
if an Army is deficient in this quality, every endeavour should
be made to simplify the operations of the War as much as
possible, or to introduce double efficiency in the organization
of the Army in some other respect, and not to expect from the

mere name of a standing Army, that which only the veritable thing itself can give.

The military virtue of an Army is therefore, one of the most important moral powers in War, and where it is wanting, we either see its place supplied by one of the others, such as the great superiority of generalship or *popular enthusiasm*, or we find the results not commensurate with the exertions made. How much that is great, this spirit, this sterling worth of an army, this refining of ore into the polished metal, has already done, we see in the history of the Macedonians under Alexander, the Roman legions under Caesar, the Spanish infantry under Alexander Farnese, the Swedes under Gustavus Adolphus and Charles XII, the Prussians under Frederick the Great, and the French under Napoleon. We must purposely shut our eyes against all historical proof, if we do not admit, that the astonishing successes of these Generals and their greatness in situations of extreme difficulty, were only possible with Armies possessing this virtue.

This spirit can only be generated from two sources, and only by these two conjointly ; the first is a succession of campaigns and great victories ; the other is, an activity of the Army carried sometimes to the highest pitch. Only by these, does the soldier learn to know his powers. The more a General is in the habit of demanding from his troops, the surer he will be that his demands will be answered. The soldier is as proud of overcoming toil, as he is of surmounting danger. Therefore it is only in the soil of incessant activity and exertion that the germ will thrive, but also only in the sunshine of victory. Once it becomes a *strong tree*, it will stand against the fiercest storms of misfortune and defeat, and even against the indolent inactivity of peace, at least for a time. It can therefore only be created in War, and under great Generals, but no doubt it may last at least for several generations, even under Generals of moderate capacity, and through considerable periods of peace.

BOLDNESS

This noble impulse, with which the human soul raises itself above the most formidable dangers, is to be regarded as an active principle peculiarly belonging to War. In fact, in what branch of human activity should boldness have a right of citizenship if not in War ?

Let us admit in fact it has in War even its own prerogatives. Over and above the result of the calculation of space, time, and quantity, we must allow a certain percentage which boldness derives from the weakness of others, whenever it gains the mastery. It is therefore, virtually, a creative power. This is not difficult to demonstrate philosophically. As often as boldness encounters hesitation, the probability of the result is of necessity in its favour, because the very state of hesitation implies a loss of equilibrium already. It is only when it encounters cautious foresight—which we may say is just as bold, at all events just as strong and powerful as itself—that it is at a disadvantage ; such cases, however, rarely occur. Out of the whole multitude of prudent men in the world, the great majority are so from timidity.

The higher the rank the more necessary it is that boldness should be accompanied by a reflective mind, that it may not be a mere blind outburst of passion to no purpose ; for with increase of rank it becomes always less a matter of self-sacrifice and more a matter of the preservation of others, and the good of the whole. Where regulations of the service, as a kind of second nature, prescribe for the masses, reflection must be the guide of the General, and in his case individual boldness in action may easily become a fault. Still, at the same time, it is a fine failing, and must not be looked at in the same light as any other. Happy the Army in which an untimely boldness frequently manifests itself ; it is an exuberant growth which shows a rich soil. Even foolhardiness, that is boldness without an object, is not to be despised. It is only when it strikes at the root of obedience, when it treats with contempt the orders of superior authority, that it must be repressed as a dangerous evil, not on its own account but on account of the act of disobedience, for there is nothing *in War* which is of *greater importance than obedience*.

One would suppose it natural that the interposition of a reasonable object should stimulate boldness, and therefore lessen its intrinsic merit, and yet the reverse is the case in reality.

The intervention of lucid thought or the general supremacy of mind deprives the emotional forces of a great part of their power. On that account *boldness becomes of rarer occurrence the higher we ascend the scale of rank.*

Almost all the Generals who are represented in history as merely having attained to mediocrity, and as wanting in decision when in supreme command, are men celebrated in their antecedent career for their boldness and decision.

In those motives to bold action which arise from the pressure of necessity we must make a distinction. Necessity has its degrees of intensity. If it lies near at hand, if the person acting is in the pursuit of his object driven into great dangers in order to escape others equally great, then we can only admire his resolution, which still has also its value. If a young man to show his skill in horsemanship leaps across a deep cleft, then he is bold ; if he makes the same leap pursued by a troop of head-chopping Janissaries he is only resolute.

Although Strategy is only the province of Generals-in-Chief or Commanders in the highest positions, still boldness in all the other branches of an Army is as little a matter of indifference to it as their other military virtues. With an Army belonging to a bold race, and in which the spirit of boldness has been always nourished, very different things may be undertaken than with one in which this virtue is unknown.

The higher we rise in a position of command, the more of the mind, understanding, and penetration predominate in activity, the more therefore is boldness, which is a property of the feelings kept in subjection, and for that reason we find it so rarely in the highest positions, but then, so much the more should it be admired. Boldness, directed by an overruling intelligence, is the stamp of the hero : this boldness does not consist in venturing directly against the nature of things, in a downright contempt of the laws of probability, but, if a choice is once made, in the rigorous adherence to that higher calculation which genius, the tact of judgment, has gone over with the speed of lightning. The more boldness lends wings to the mind and the discernment, so much the farther they will reach in their flight, so much the more comprehensive will be the view, the more exact the result, but certainly always only in the sense that with greater objects greater dangers are connected.

We think then that it is impossible to imagine a distinguished General without boldness, that is to say, that no man can become

one who is not born with this power of the soul, and we therefore look upon it as the first requisite for such a career. How
much of this inborn power, developed and moderated through
education and the circumstances of life, is left when the man
has attained a high position, is the second question. The greater
this power still is, the stronger will genius be on the wing, the
higher will be its flight. The risks become always greater, but
the purpose grows with them.

We have still to advert to one very important circumstance.

The spirit of boldness can exist in an Army, either because
it is in the people, or because it has been generated in a successful
War conducted by able Generals. In the latter case it must of
course be dispensed with at the commencement.

Now in our days there is hardly any other means of educating
the spirit of a people in this respect, except by War, and that
too under bold Generals. By it alone can that effeminacy of
feeling be counteracted, that propensity to seek for the enjoyment of comfort, which cause degeneracy in a people rising in
prosperity and immersed in an extremely busy commerce.

A Nation can hope to have a strong position in the political
world only if its character and practice in actual War mutually
support each other in constant reciprocal action.

In the matter of *Perseverance* the reader expects to hear of
angles and lines, and finds, instead of these citizens of the scientific
world, only people out of common life, such as he meets with
every day in the street. And yet the author cannot make up
his mind to become a hair's breadth more mathematical than
the subject seems to him to require, and he is not alarmed at the
surprise which the reader may show.

In War more than anywhere else in the world things happen
differently to what we had expected, and look differently when
near, to what they did at a distance. With what serenity the
architect can watch his work gradually rising and growing into
his plan. The doctor although much more at the mercy of
mysterious agencies and chances than the architect, still knows
enough of the forms and effects of his means. In War, on the
other hand, the Commander of an immense whole finds himself in a constant whirlpool of false and true information, of
mistakes committed through fear, through negligence, through
precipitation, of contraventions of his authority, either from

mistaken or correct motives, from ill will, true or false sense of duty, indolence or exhaustion, of accidents which no mortal could have foreseen. In short, he is the victim of a hundred thousand impressions, of which the most have an intimidating, the fewest an encouraging tendency. By long experience in War, the tact is acquired of readily appreciating the value of these incidents; high courage and stability of character stand proof against them, as the rock resists the beating of the waves. He who would yield to these impressions would never carry out an undertaking, and on that account *perseverance* in the proposed object, as long as there is no decided reason against it, is a most necessary counterpoise. Further, there is hardly any celebrated enterprise in War which was not achieved by endless exertion, pains, and privations; and as here the weakness of the physical and moral man is ever disposed to yield, only an immense force of will, which manifests itself in perseverance admired by present and future generations, can conduct us to our goal.

SUPERIORITY OF NUMBERS

This is in tactics, as well as in Strategy, the most general principle of victory, and will be examined by us first in its generality, for which we may be permitted the following exposition:

Strategy fixes the point where, the time when, and the numerical force with which the battle is to be fought. By this triple determination it has therefore a very essential influence on the issue of the combat. If tactics has fought the battle, if the result is over, let it be victory or defeat, Strategy makes such use of it as can be made in accordance with the great object of the War.

Those things through which Strategy has an influence on the issue of the combat, inasmuch as it establishes the same, to a certain extent decrees them, are not so simple that they can be embraced in one single view. For as Strategy appoints time, place and force, it can do so in practice in many ways, each of which influences in a different manner the result of the combat as well as its consequences. Therefore we shall only get acquainted with this also by degrees, that is, through the subjects which more closely determine the application.

If we strip the combat of all modifications which it may undergo according to its immediate purpose and the circumstances from which it proceeds, lastly if we set aside the valour of the troops, because that is a given quantity, then there remains only the bare conception of the combat, that is a combat without form, in which we distinguish nothing but the number of the combatants.

This number will therefore determine victory. Now from the number of things above deducted to get to this point, it is shown that the superiority in numbers in a battle is only one of the factors employed to produce victory : that therefore so far from having with the superiority in number obtained all, or even only the principal thing, we have perhaps got very little by it, according as the other circumstances which co-operate happen to vary.

But this superiority has degrees, it may be imagined as twofold, threefold or fourfold, and every one sees, that by increasing in this way, it must (at last) overpower everything else.

In such an aspect we grant, that the superiority in numbers is the most important factor in the result of a combat, only it must be sufficiently great to be a counterpoise to all the other co-operating circumstances. *The direct result of this is, that the greatest possible number of troops should be brought into action at the decisive point.*

Whether the troops thus brought are sufficient or not, we have then done in this respect all that our means allowed. This is the first principle in Strategy, therefore in general as now stated, it is just as well suited for Greeks and Persians, or for Englishmen and Mahrattas, as for French and Germans.

There only remains a difference in the military virtue of Armies, and in the talent of Generals which may fluctuate with time from side to side. If we go through the military history of modern Europe, we find no example of a Marathon.[1]

Frederick the Great beat 80,000 Austrians at Leuthen with about 30,000 men, and at Rosbach with 25,000 some 50,000 allies ; these are, however, the only instances of victories gained against an enemy double, or more than double in numbers.

We think, that under our conditions, as well as in all similar

---

[1] At Marathon (490 B.C.) ten thousand Athenians led by Miltiades defeated a Persian Army of 40,000 to 60,000.—Ed.

ones, the superiority at the decisive point is a matter of capital importance, and that this subject, in the generality of cases, is decidedly the most important of all. The strength at the decisive point depends on the absolute strength of the Army, and on skill in making use of it.

The first rule is therefore to enter the field with an Army as strong as possible. This sounds very like a commonplace, but it is really not so.

In order to show that for a long time the strength of forces was by no means regarded as a chief point, we need only observe, that in most, and even in the most detailed histories of the Wars in the eighteenth century, the strength of the Armies is either not given at all, or only incidentally, and in no case is any special value laid upon it.

Another proof lies in a wonderful notion which haunted the heads of many critical historians, according to which there was a certain size of an Army which was the best, a normal strength, beyond which the forces in excess were burdensome rather than serviceable.

Lastly, there are a number of instances to be found, in which all the available forces were not really brought into the battle,[1] or into the War, because the superiority of numbers was not considered to have that importance which in the nature of things belongs to it.

The measure of the absolute force with which the War is to be conducted is determined by the Government ; and although with this determination the real action of War commences, and it forms an essential part of the Strategy of the War, still in most cases the General who is to command these forces in the War must regard their absolute strength as a given quantity, whether it be that he has had no voice in fixing it, or that circumstances prevented a sufficient expansion being given to it.

There remains nothing, therefore, where an absolute superiority is not attainable, but to produce a *relative* one at the decisive point, by making skilful use of what we have.

The calculation of space and time appears as the most essential thing to this end—and this has caused that subject to be regarded as one which embraces nearly the whole art of using military forces.

[1] By Wellington at Waterloo.

But the calculation of time and space, although it lies universally at the foundation of Strategy, and is to a certain extent its daily bread, is still neither the most difficult, nor the most decisive one.

The right appreciation of their opponents, the audacity to leave for a short space of time a small force only before them, energy in forced marches, boldness in sudden attacks, the intensified activity which great souls acquire in the moment of danger, these are the grounds of victories ; and what have these to do with the ability to make an exact calculation of two such simple things as time and space ?

Much more frequently the relative superiority—that is, the skilful assemblage of superior forces at the decisive point—has its foundation in the right appreciation of those points, in the judicious direction which by that means has been given to the forces from the very first, and in the resolution required to sacrifice the unimportant to the advantage of the important—that is, to keep the forces concentrated in an overpowering mass. In this, Frederick the Great and Napoleon are particularly characteristic.

We think we have now allotted to the superiority in numbers the importance which belongs to it ; it is to be regarded as the fundamental idea, always to be aimed at before all and as far as possible.

But to regard it on this account as a necessary condition of victory would be a complete misconception of our exposition ; in the conclusion to be drawn from it there lies nothing more than the value which should attach to numerical strength in the combat. If that strength is made as great as possible, then the maxim is satisfied ; a review of the total relations must then decide whether or not the combat is to be avoided for want of sufficient force.

THE SURPRISE

From the subject of the foregoing chapter, the general endeavour to attain a relative superiority, there follows another endeavour which must consequently be just as general in its nature : this is the *surprise* of the enemy. It lies more or less at the foundation of all undertakings, for without it the preponderance at the decisive point is not properly conceivable.

The surprise is, therefore, not only the means to the attainment of numerical superiority ; but it is also to be regarded as a substantive principle in itself, on account of its moral effect. When it is successful in a high degree, confusion and broken courage in the enemy's ranks are the consequences ; and of the degree to which these multiply a success, there are examples enough, great and small. We are not now speaking of the particular surprise which belongs to the attack, but of the endeavour by measures generally, and especially by the distribution of forces, to surprise the enemy, which can be imagined just as well in the defensive, and which in the tactical defence particularly is a chief point.

We say, surprise lies at the foundation of all undertakings without exception, only in very different degrees according to the nature of the undertaking and other circumstances.

This difference, indeed, originates in the properties or peculiarities of the Army and its Commander, in those even of the Government.

Secrecy and rapidity are the two factors in this product ; and these suppose in the Government and the Commander-in-Chief great energy, and on the part of the Army a high sense of military duty. With effeminacy and loose principles it is in vain to calculate upon a surprise. But so general, indeed so indispensable, as is this endeavour, and true as it is that it is never wholly unproductive of effect, still it is not the less true that it seldom succeeds to a *remarkable* degree, and this follows from the nature of the idea itself. We should form an erroneous conception if we believed that by this means chiefly there is much to be attained in War. In idea it promises a great deal ; in the execution it generally sticks fast by the friction of the whole machine.

In tactics the surprise is much more at home, for the very natural reason that all times and spaces are on a smaller scale. It will, therefore, in Strategy be the more feasible in proportion as the measures lie nearer to the province of tactics, and more difficult the higher up they lie towards the province of policy.

It rarely happens that one State surprises another by a War, or by the direction which it gives the mass of its forces. In the seventeenth and eighteenth centuries, when War turned very much upon sieges, it was a frequent ain, and quite a peculiar and important chapter in the Art of War, to invest a strong place unexpectedly, but even that only rarely succeeded.

On the other hand, with things which can be done in a day or two, a surprise is much more conceivable,[1] and, therefore, also it is often not difficult thus to gain a march upon the enemy, and thereby a position, a point of country, a road, etc. But it is evident that what surprise gains in this way in easy execution, it loses in the efficacy, as the greater the efficacy the greater always the difficulty of execution. Whoever thinks that with such surprises on a small scale, he may connect great results— as, for example, the gain of a battle, the capture of an imporant magazine—believes in something which it is certainly very possible to imagine, but for which there is no warrant in history ; for there are upon the whole very few instances where anything great has resulted from such surprises ; from which we may justly conclude that inherent difficulties lie in the way of their success.

But we by no means deny that there can be success ; we only connect with it *a necessity of favourable circumstances*, which, certainly do not occur very frequently, and which the Commander can seldom bring about himself.

Two Generals afford each a striking illustration of this. We take first Napoleon in his famous enterprise against Blücher's Army in February, 1814, when it was separated from the Grand Army, and descending the Marne. It would not be easy to find a two days' march to surprise the enemy productive of greater results than this ; Blücher's Army, extended over a distance of three days' march, was beaten in detail, and suffered a loss nearly equal to that of defeat in a great battle. This was completely the effect of a surprise, for if Blücher had thought of such a near possibility of an attack from Napoleon he would have organized his march quite differently. To this mistake of Blücher's the result is to be attributed. Napoleon did not know all these circumstances, and so there was a piece of good fortune that mixed itself up in his favour.

It is the same with the battle of Liegnitz, 1760. Frederick the Great gained this fine victory through altering during the night a position which he had just before taken up. Laudon was through this completely surprised, and lost 70 pieces of artillery

[1] *E.g.* Pearl Harbour.—Ed.

and 10,000 men. Although Frederick the Great had at this time adopted the principle of moving backwards and forwards in order to make a battle impossible, or at least to disconcert the enemy's plans, still the alteration of position on the night of the 14–15 was not made exactly with that intention, but as the King himself says, because the position of the 14th did not please him. Here, therefore, chance was hard at work ; without this happy conjunction of the attack and the change of position in the night, and the difficult nature of the country, the result would not have been the same.

Also in the higher and highest province of Strategy there are some instances of surprises fruitful in results. We shall only cite the celebrated passage of the Alps by Napoleon in 1800, and, as an instance of a War wholly unexpected, we may bring forward the invasion of Silesia by Frederick the Great. Great and powerful are here the results everywhere, but such events are not common in history if we do not confuse with them cases in which a State, for want of activity and energy (Russia, 1812), has not completed its preparations in time.

ASSEMBLY OF FORCES IN SPACE AND TIME

The best Strategy is *always to be very strong*, first generally, then at the decisive point. Therefore, apart from the energy which creates the Army, a work which is not always done by the General, there is no more imperative and no simpler law for Strategy than to *keep the forces concentrated*.—No portion is to be separated from the main body unless called away by some urgent necessity. On this maxim we stand firm, and look upon it as a guide to be depended upon. What are the reasonable grounds on which a detachment of forces may be made we shall learn by degrees. Then we shall also see that this principle cannot have the same general effects in every War, but that these are different according to the means and end.

It seems incredible, and yet it has happened a hundred times, that troops have been divided and separated merely through a mysterious feeling of conventional manner, without any clear perception of the reason.

If the concentration of the whole force is acknowledged as the norm, and every division and separation as an exception which must be justified, then not only will that folly be completely avoided, but also many an erroneous ground for separating troops will be barred admission.

War is the shock of two opposing forces in collision with each other, from which it follows as a matter of course that the stronger not only destroys the other, but carries it forward with it in its movement. This fundamentally admits of no successive action of powers, but makes the simultaneous application of all forces intended for the shock appear as a primordial law of War.

So it is in reality, but only so far as the struggle resembles also in practice a mechanical shock. But when it consists in a lasting mutual action of destructive forces, then we can certainly imagine a successive action of forces. This is the case in tactics, principally because firearms form the basis of all tactics, but also for other reasons as well. If in a fire combat 1000 men are opposed to 500, then the gross loss is calculated from the amount of the enemy's force and our own ; 1000 men fire twice as many shots as 500, but more shots will take effect on the 1000 than on the 500 because it is assumed that they stand in closer order than the other. If we were to suppose the number of hits to be double, then the losses on each side would be equal. From the 500 there would be for example 200 disabled, and out of the body of 1000 likewise the same ; now if the 500 had kept another body of equal number quite out of fire, then both sides would have 800 effective men ; but of these, on the one side there would be 500 men quite fresh, fully supplied with ammunition, and in their full vigour ; on the other side only 800 all alike shaken in their order, in want of sufficient ammunition and weakened in physical force.

In this way it becomes evident how the employment of too many forces in combat may be disadvantageous ; for whatever advantages the superiority may give in the first moment, we may have to pay dearly for in the next.

But this danger only endures as long as the disorder, the state of confusion and weakness lasts, in a word, up to the crisis which every combat brings with it even for the conqueror. Within the duration of this relaxed state of exhaustion, the appearance of a proportionate number of fresh troops is decisive.

But when this disordering effect of victory stops, and therefore only the moral superiority remains which every victory gives, then it is no longer possible for fresh troops to restore the combat, they would only be carried along in the general movement ; a beaten Army cannot be brought back to victory a day after by means of a strong reserve. Here we find ourselves at the source of a highly material difference between *tactics* and *strategy*.

The *tactical* results, the results within the four corners of the battle, and before its close, lie for the most part within the limits of that period of disorder and weakness. But the *strategic* result, that is to say, the result of the total combat, of the victories realized, let them be small or great, lies completely (beyond) outside of that period.

The consequence of this difference is that tactics can make a continued use of forces, Strategy only a simultaneous one.

If I cannot, in tactics, decide all by the first success, if I have to fear the next moment, it follows of itself that I employ only so much of my force for the success of the first moment as appears sufficient for that object, and keep the rest beyond the reach of fire or conflict of any kind. But it is not so in Strategy. Partly, as we have just shown, it has not so much reason to fear a reaction after a success realized, because with that success the crisis stops ; partly all the forces strategically employed are not necessarily weakened. Only so much of them as have been tactically in conflict with the enemy's force, that is, engaged in partial combat, are weakened by it.

If, therefore, in Strategy the loss does not increase with the number of the troops employed, then it follows naturally that in Strategy we can never employ too many forces, and consequently also that they must be applied simultaneously to the immediate purpose.

But we must vindicate this proposition upon another ground.

Fatigue, exertion, and privation constitute in War a special principle of destruction, not essentially belonging to contest, but more or less inseparably bound up with it, and certainly one which especially belongs to Strategy. It is not at all uncommon for a victorious Army to lose many more by sickness than on the field of battle.

If, therefore, we look at this sphere of destruction in Strategy in the same manner as we have considered that of fire and close combat in tactics, then we may well imagine that everything which comes within its vortex will, at the end of the campaign or of any other stragetic period, be reduced to a state of weakness, which makes the arrival of a fresh force decisive. We might therefore conclude that there is a motive in the one case as well as the other to strive for the first success with as few forces as possible, in order to keep up this fresh force for the last.

This point being settled, then the question is, Do the losses which a force sustains through fatigues and privations increase in proportion to the size of the force, as is the case in a combat ? And to that we answer " No."

The fatigues of War result in a great measure from the dangers with which every moment of the act of War is more or less impregnated. To encounter these dangers at all points gives employment to a multitude of agencies, which make up the tactical and strategic service of the Army. This service is more difficult the weaker an Army is, and easier as its numerical superiority over that of the enemy increases. Who can doubt this ? A campaign against a much weaker enemy will therefore cost smaller efforts than against one just as strong or stronger.

So much for the fatigues. It is somewhat different with the privations ; they consist chiefly of two things, the want of food, and the want of shelter for the troops, either in quarters or in suitable camps. Both these wants will no doubt be greater in proportion as the number of men on one spot is greater. But does not the superiority in force afford also the best means of spreading out and finding more room, and therefore more means of subsistence and shelter ?

If Napoleon, in his invasion of Russia in 1812, concentrated his Army in great masses upon one single road in a manner never heard of before, and thus caused privations equally unparalleled, we must ascribe it to his maxim *that it is impossible to be too strong at the decisive point.* Whether in this instance he did not strain the principle too far is a question which would be out of place here ; but it is certain that, if he had made a point of avoiding the distress which was by that means brought about, he had only to advance on a greater breadth of front. Room was not wanted for the purpose in Russia, and in very few cases can it be wanted.

But there still remains a most important point to be noticed. In a partial combat, the force required to obtain a great result can be approximately estimated without much difficulty. In Strategy this may be said to be impossible, because the strategic result has no such well-defined object and no such circumscribed limits as the tactical. Thus what can be looked upon in tactics as an excess of power must be regarded in Strategy as a means to give expansion to success.

By means of his enormous numerical superiority, Napoleon was enabled to reach Moscow in 1812, and to take that central capital. Had he by means of this superiority succeeded in completely defeating the Russian Army, he would, in all probability, have concluded a peace in Moscow which in any other way was much less attainable. This example is used to explain the idea, not to prove it.

All these reflections bear merely upon the idea of a successive employment of forces, and not upon the conception of a reserve properly so called, which they, no doubt, come in contact with throughout, but which, as we shall see in the following chapter, is connected with some other considerations.

What we desire to establish here is, that if in tactics time appears as a factor in the result, this is not the case in Strategy in a material degree. The destructive effects which are also produced upon the forces in Strategy by time, are partly diminished through their mass, partly made good in other ways.

Therefore, all forces which are available and destined for a strategic object should be *simultaneously* applied to it ; and this application will be so much the more complete the more everything is compressed into one act and into one movement.

We now turn to a subject very closely connected with our present considerations, which must be settled before full light can be thrown on the whole, we mean the *strategic reserve*.

STRATEGIC RESERVE

A reserve has two objects which are very distinct from each other, namely, first, the prolongation and renewal of the combat, and secondly, for use in case of unforeseen events. The first object implies the utility of a successive application of forces, and on that account cannot occur in Strategy. Cases in which a corps is sent to succour a point which is supposed to be about fall are plainly to be placed in the category of the second object.

But the necessity for a force ready for unforeseen events may also take place in Strategy, and consequently there may also be a strategic reserve, but only where unforeseen events are imaginable. In tactics, where the enemy's measures are generally first ascertained by direct sight, and where they may be concealed by every wood, every fold of undulating ground, we must naturally always be alive, more or less, to the possibility of unforeseen events.

Such cases must also happen in Strategy, because the strategic act is directly linked to the tactical. In Strategy also many a measure is first adopted in consequnce of what is actually seen, or in consequence of uncertain reports arriving from day to day, or even from hour to hour, and lastly, from the actual results of the combats ; it is, therefore, an essential condition of strategic command that, according to the degree of uncertainty, forces must be kept in reserve against future contingencies.

In the defensive generally, but particularly in the defence of certain obstacles of ground, like rivers, hills, etc., such contingencies, as is well known, happen constantly.

But this uncertainty diminishes in proportion as the strategic activity has less of the tactical character, and ceases almost altogether in those regions where it borders on politics.

We find strategic reserves always more superfluous, always more useless, always more dangerous, the more general their destination.

The point where the idea of a strategic reserve begins to become inconsistent is not difficult to determine : it lies in the *supreme decision*. Employment must be given to all the forces within the space of the supreme decision, and every reserve (active force available) which is only intended for use after that decision is opposed to common sense.

If, therefore, tactics has in its reserves the means of not only meeting unforeseen dispositions on the part of the enemy, but also of repairing that which never can be foreseen, the result of the combat, should that be unfortunate ; Strategy on the other hand must at least as far as relates to the capital result, renounce the use of these means. As a rule, it can only repair the losses sustained at one point by advantages gained at another, in a few cases by moving troops from one point to another ; the idea of preparing for such reverses by placing forces in reserve beforehand, can never be entertained in Strategy.

ECONOMY OF FORCES

The road of reason, as we have said, seldom allows itself to be reduced to a mathematical line by principles and opinions. There remains always a certain margin. But it is the same in all the practical arts of life. For the lines of beauty there are no abscissæ and ordinates ; circles and ellipses are not described by means of their algebraical formulæ. The actor in War therefore soon finds he must trust himself to the delicate tact of judgment which, founded on natural quickness of perception, and educated by reflection, almost unconsciously seizes upon the right ; he soon finds that at one time he must simplify the law (by reducing it) to some prominent characteristic points which form his rules ; that at another the adopted method must become the staff on which he leans.

As one of these simplified characteristic points, we look upon the principle of watching continually over the co-operation of all forces, or in other words, of keeping constantly in view that no part of them should ever be idle. Whoever has forces where the enemy does not give them sufficient employment, whoever has part of his forces on the march—that is, allows them to lie dead—while the enemy's are fighting, he is a bad manager of his forces. In this sense there is a waste of forces, which is even worse than their employment to no purpose. If there must be action, then the first point is that all parts act, because the most purposeless activity still keeps employed and destroys a portion of the enemy's force, while troops completely inactive are for the moment quite neutralized. Unmistakably this idea is bound up with the principles contained in the last three chapters, it is the same truth, but seen from a somewhat more comprehensive point of view and condensed into a single conception.

ON THE SUSPENSION OF THE ACT IN WARFARE

If one considers War as an act of mutual destruction, we must of necessity imagine both parties as making some progress ; but at the same time, as regards the existing moment, we must almost as necessarily suppose the one party in a state of expectation, and only the other actually advancing, for circumstances can never be actually the same on both sides, or continue so. In time a change must ensue, from which it follows that the present moment is more favourable to one side than the other. Now if we suppose that both commanders have a full knowledge of this circumstance, then the one has a motive for action, which at the same time is a motive for the other to wait ; therefore, according to this it cannot be for the interest of both at the same time to advance, nor can waiting be for the interest of both at the same time.

But even if we suppose the possibility of a perfect equality of circumstances in this respect, or if we take into account that through imperfect knowledge of their mutual position such an equality may appear to the two Commanders to subsist, still the difference of political objects does away with this possibility of suspension. One of the parties must of necessity be assumed politically from defensive intentions on both sides. To the first then belongs the positive action, for it is only by that means that he can attain the positive object ; therefore, in cases where both parties are in precisely similar circumstances, the aggressor is called upon to act by virtue of his positive object.

If we cast a glance at military history in general, we find so much the opposite of an incessant advance towards the aim, that *standing still* and *doing nothing* is quite plainly the *normal condition* of an Army in the midst of War, *acting*, the *exception*. This must almost raise a doubt as to the correctness of our conception.

How could anyone in fact justify in the eyes of reason the expenditure of forces in War, if acting was not the object ? The baker only heats his oven if he has bread to put into it ; the horse is only yoked to the carriage if we mean to drive ; why then make the enormous effort of a War if we look for nothing else by it but like efforts on the part of the enemy ?

So much in justification of the general principle ; now as to its modifications, as far as they lie in the nature of the thing and are independent of special cases.

There are three causes to be noticed here, which appear as innate counterpoises and prevent the over-rapid or uncontrollable movement of the wheel-work.

The first, which produces a constant tendency to delay, and is thereby a retarding principle, is the natural timidity and want of resolution in the human mind, a kind of inertia in the moral world, which is produced not by attractive, but by repellent forces, that is to say, by dread of danger and responsibility.

The mere idea of the object for which arms have been taken up is seldom sufficient to overcome this resistant force, and if a warlike enterprising spirit is not at the head, who feels himself in War in his natural element, as much as a fish in the ocean, or if there is not the pressure from above of some great responsibility, then standing still will be the order of the day, and progress will be the exception.

The second cause is the imperfection of human perception and judgment, which is greater in War than anywhere, because a person hardly knows exactly his own position from one moment to another, and can only conjecture on slight grounds that of the enemy, which is purposely concealed ; this often gives rise to the case of both parties looking upon one and the same object as advantageous for them, while in reality the interest of one must preponderate ; thus then each may think he acts wisely by waiting another moment.

The third cause which catches hold, like a ratchet wheel in machinery, from time to time producing a complete standstill, is the greater strength of the defensive form. A may feel too weak to attack B, from which it does not follow that B is strong enough for an attack on A. Therefore it may so happen that both parties, at one and the same time, not only feel themselves too weak to attack, but also are so in reality.

Thus even in the midst of the act of War itself, anxious sagacity and the apprehension of too great danger find vantage ground, by means of which they can exert their power, and tame the elementary impetuosity of War.

These things may obtain such a preponderating influence as to make of War a half-and-half affair. A War is often nothing more than an armed neutrality, or a menacing attitude to support negotiations or an attempt to gain some small advantage by small erections.

The result of all causes now adduced is that the hostile action of a campaign does not progress by a continuous, but by an intermittent movement, and that, therefore, between the separate bloody acts, there is a period of watching, during which both parties fall into the defensive, and also that usually a higher object causes the principle of aggression to predominate on one side, and thus leaves it in general in an advancing position, by which then its proceedings become modified in some degree.

TENSION AND REST

The Dynamic Law of War

We have seen how, in most campaigns, much more time used to be spent in standing still and inaction than in activity. Now, although, as observed in the preceding chapter we see quite a different character in the present form of War, still it is certain that real action will always be interrupted more or less by long pauses ; and this leads to the necessity of our examining more closely the nature of these two phases of War.

If there is a suspension of action in War, that is, if neither party wills something positive, there is rest, and consequently equilibrium, but certainly an equilibrium in the largest signification, in which not only the moral and physical war-forces, but all relations and interests, come into calculation. As soon as ever one of the two parties proposes to himself a new positive object, and commences active steps towards it, even if it is only by preparations, and as soon as the adversary opposes this, there is a tension of powers ; this lasts until the decision takes place—that is, until one party either gives up his object or the other has conceded it to him.

This decision—the foundation of which lies always in the combat-combinations which are made on each side—is followed by a movement in one or other direction.

When this movement has exhausted itself, either in the difficulties which had to be mastered, in overcoming its own internal triction, or through new resistant forces prepared by the acts of the enemy, then either a state of rest takes place or a new tension with a decision, and then a new movement, in most cases in the opposite direction.

This speculative distinction between equilibrium, tension

and motion is more essential for practical action than may at first sight appear.

In a state of rest and of equilibrium a varied kind of activity may prevail on one side that results from opportunity, and does not aim at a great alteration. Such an activity may contain important combats—even pitched battles—but yet it is still of quite a different nature, and on that account generally different in its effects.

If a state of *tension* exists, the effects of the decision are always greater partly because a greater force of will and a greater pressure of circumstances manifest themselves therein ; partly because everything has been prepared and arranged for a great movement. The decision in such cases resembles the effect of a mine well closed and tamped, whilst an event in itself perhaps just as great, in a state of *rest*, is more or less like a mass of powder puffed away in the open air.

At the same time, as a matter of course, the state of tension must be imagined in different degrees of intensity, and it may therefore approach gradually by many steps towards the state of rest, so that at the last there is a very slight difference between them.

Now the real use which we derive from these reflections is the conclusion that *every measure which is taken during a state of tension is more important and more prolific in results than the same measure could be in a state of equilibrium*, and that this importance increases immensely in the highest degrees of tension.

In a tract of country which the enemy abandons to us because he cannot defend it, we can settle ourselves differently from what we should do if the retreat of the enemy was only made with the view to a decision under more favourable circumstances. Again, a strategic attack in course of execution, a faulty position, a single false march, may be decisive in its consequence ; whilst in a state of equilibrium such errors must be of a very glaring kind, even to excite the activity of the enemy in a general way.

Most bygone Wars, as we have already said, consisted, so far as regards the greater part of the time, in this state of equilibrium, or at least in such short tensions with long intervals between them, and weak in their effects, that the events to which they gave rise were seldom great successes, often they were theatrical exhibitions, got up in honour of a royal birthday (Hochkirch), often a mere satisfying of the honour of the arms (Kundersdorf), or the personal vanity of the commander (Freiberg).

That a Commander should thoroughly understand these states, that he should have the tact to act in the spirit of them, we hold to be a great requisite, and we have had experience in the campaign of 1806 [1] how far it is sometimes wanting. In that tremendous tension, when everything pressed on towards a supreme decision, and that alone with all its consequences should have occupied the whole soul of the Commander, measures were proposed and even partly carried out (such as the reconnaissance towards Franconia), which at the most might have given a kind of gentle play of oscillation within a state of equilibrium. Over these blundering schemes and views, absorbing the activity of the Army, the really necessary means, which could alone save, were lost sight of.

But this speculative distinction which we have made is also necessary for our further progress in the construction of our theory, because all that we have to say on the relation of attack and defence, and on the completion of this double-sided act, concerns the state of the crisis in which the forces are placed during the tension and motion, and because all the activity which can take place during the condition of equilibrium can only be regarded and treated as a corollary ; for that crisis is the real War and this state of equilibrium only its reflection.

THE COMBAT

The Combat in General

Combat means fighting, and in this the destruction or conquest of the enemy is the object, and the enemy, in the particular combat, is the armed force which stands opposed to us.

If we suppose the State and its military force as a unit, then the most natural idea is to imagine the War also as one great combat. But our Wars are made up of a number of great and small simultaneous or consecutive combats, and this severance

---

[1] As aide-de-camp to Prince Augustus of Prussia, Clausewitz was wounded and taken prisoner by Napoleon.—Ed.

of the activity into so many separate actions is owing to the great
multiplicity of the relations out of which War arises with us.

In point of fact, the ultimate object of our Wars, the political
one, is not always quite a simple one ; and even were it so,
still the action is bound up with such a number of conditions
and considerations to be taken into account, that the object can
no longer be attained by one single great act but only through
a number of greater or smaller acts which are bound up into a
whole ; each of these separate acts is therefore a part of a whole,
and has consequently a special object by which it is bound to
this whole.

What is overcoming the enemy ? Invariably the destruction
of his military force, whether it be by death, or wounds, or any
means ; whether it be completely or only to such a degree that
he can no longer continue the contest ; therefore as long as we
set aside all special objects of combats, we may look upon the
complete or partial destruction of the enemy as the only object
of all combats.

Now we maintain that in the majority of cases, and especially
in great battles, the special object by which the battle is in-
dividualized and bound up with the great whole is only a weak
modification of that general object, important enough to
individualize the battle, but always insignificant in comparison
with that general object. If this assertion is correct, then we see
that the idea, according to which the destruction of the enemy's
force is only the means, and something else always the object,
can only be true in form, but, that it would lead to false conclusions if we did not recollect that this destruction of the enemy's
force is comprised in that object, and that this object is only
a weak modification of it.

But now how shall we manage to show that in most cases,
and in those of most importance, the destruction of the enemy's
Army is the chief thing ? How shall we manage to combat
that extremely subtle idea, which supposes it possible, through
the use of a special artificial form, to effect by a small direct
destruction of the enemy's forces a much greater destruction
indirectly, or by means of small but extremely well-directed
blows to produce such paralyzation of the enemy's forces, such
a command over the enemy's will, that this mode of proceeding
is to be viewed as a great shortening of the road ? Undoubtedly

a victory at one point may be of more value than at another. Undoubtedly there is a scientific arrangement of battles amongst themselves, even in Strategy, which is in fact nothing but the Art of thus arranging them. To deny that is not our intention, but we assert that the direct destruction of the enemy's forces is everywhere predominant ; we contend here for the over-ruling importance of this destructive principle and nothing else.

We must, however, call to mind that we are now engaged with Strategy, not with tactics, and that our assertion is that only great tactical results can lead to great strategical ones, or, as we have already once before more distinctly expressed it, *the tactical successes* are of paramount importance in the conduct of War.

The proof of this assertion seems to us simple enough ; it lies in the time which every complicated (artificial) combination requires. The question whether a simple attack, or one more carefully prepared, *i.e.*, more artificial, will produce greater effects, may undoubtedly be decided in favour of the latter as long as the enemy is assumed to remain quite passive. But every carefully combined attack requires time for its prepara-tion, and if a counter-stroke by the enemy intervenes, our whole design may be upset. Now if the enemy should decide upon some simple attack, which can be executed in a shorter time, then he gains the initiative, and destroys the effect of the great plan. Therefore, together with the expediency of a com-plicated attack we must consider all the dangers which we run during its preparation, and should only adopt it if there is no reason to fear that the enemy will disconcert our scheme. Whenever this is the case we must ourselves choose the simpler, *i.e.*, quicker way, and lower our views in this sense as far as the character, the relations of the enemy, and other circumstances may render necessary. If we quit the weak impressions of abstract ideas and descend to the region of practical life, then it is evident that a bold, courageous, resolute enemy will not let us have time for wide-reaching skilful combinations, and it is just against such a one we should require skill the most. By this it appears to us that the advantage of simple and direct results over those that are complicated is conclusively shown.

If we seek for the lowest foundation-stones of these converse propositions we find that in the one it is ability, in the other, courage. Now, there is something very attractive in the notion that a moderate degree of courage joined to great ability will produce greater effects than moderate ability with great courage. But unless we suppose these elements in a disproportionate relation, not logical, we have no right to assign to ability this advantage over courage in a field which is called danger and, which must be regarded as the true domain of courage.

After this abstract view we shall only add that experience, very far from leading to a different conclusion, is rather the sole cause which has impelled us in this direction, and given rise to such reflections.

Whoever reads history with a mind free from prejudice cannot fail to arrive at a conviction that of all military virtues, energy in the conduct of operations has always contributed the most to the glory and success of arms.

What are we now to understand by destruction of the enemy's Army? A diminution of it relatively greater than that on our own side. If we have a great superiority in numbers over the enemy, then naturally the same absolute amount of loss on both sides is for us a smaller one than for him, and consequently may be regarded in itself as an advantage.

If by a skilful disposition we have reduced our opponent to such a dilemma, that he cannot continue the combat without danger, and after some resistance he retires, then we may say, that we have conquered him at that point ; but if in this victory we have expended just as many forces as the enemy, then in closing the account of the campaign, there is no gain remaining from this victory, if such a result can be called a victory. There remains nothing over except the direct gain which we have made in the process of destruction ; but to this belong not only the losses which have taken place in the course of the combat, but also those which, after the withdrawal of the conquered part, take place as direct consequences of the same.

Now it is known by experience, that the losses in physical forces in the course of a battle seldom present a great difference between victor and vanquished respectively, and that the most decisive losses on the side of the vanquished only commence with the retreat. The weak remains of battalions already in disorder are cut down by cavalry, exhausted men strew the ground, disabled guns and broken caissons are abandoned, others in the bad stage of the roads cannot be removed quickly enough, and are captured by the enemy's troops, during the night numbers lose their way, and fall defenseless into the enemy's hands, and thus the victory mostly gains bodily substance after it is already decided. Here would be a paradox, if it did not solve itself in the following manner.

The loss in physical force is not the only one which the two sides suffer in the course of the combat ; the moral forces also are shaken, broken, and go to ruin. It is not only the loss in men, horses and guns, but in order, courage, confidence, cohesion and plan, which come into consideration when it is a question whether the fight can be still continued or not. It is principally the moral forces which decide here, and in all cases in which the conqueror has lost as heavily as the conquered, it is these alone.

The comparative relation of the physical losses is difficult to estimate in a battle, but not so the relation of the moral ones. Two things principally make it known. The one is the loss of the ground on which the fight has taken place, the other the superiority of the enemy's reserve. The more our reserves have diminished as compared with those of the enemy, the more force we have used to maintain the equilibrium ; in this at once, an evident proof of the moral superiority of the enemy is given. But the principal thing is, that men who have been engaged for a long continuance of time are more or less like burnt-out cinders ; their ammunition is consumed ; they have melted away to a certain extent ; physical and moral energies are exhausted, perhaps their courage is broken as well. Such a force, irrespective of the diminution in its number, if viewed as an organic whole, is very different from what it was before the combat ; and thus it is that the loss of moral force may be measured by the reserves that have been used as if it were on a foot-rule.

Every combat is therefore the bloody and destructive measuring of the strength of forces, physical and moral ; whoever at the close has the greatest amount of both left is the conqueror.

In the combat the loss of moral force is the chief cause of the decision ; after that is given, this loss continues to increase until it reaches its culminating-point at the close of the whole act. This then is the opportunity the victor should seize to reap his harvest by the utmost possible restrictions of his enemy's forces, the real object of engaging in the combat. On the beaten side, the loss of all order and control often makes the prolongation of resistance by individual units, by the further punishment they are certain to suffer, more injurious than useful to the whole. The spirit of the mass is broken ; the original excitement about losing or winning, through which danger was forgotten, is spent, and to the majority danger now appears no longer an appeal to their courage, but rather the endurance of a cruel punishment. Thus the instrument in the first moment of the enemy's victory is weakened and blunted, and therefore no longer fit to repay danger by danger.

This period, however, passes ; the moral forces of the conquered will recover by degrees, order will be restored, courage will revive, and in the majority of cases there remains only a small part of the superiority obtained, often none at all. In some cases, even, although rarely, the spirit of revenge and intensified hostility may bring about an opposite result. On the other hand, *whatever is gained in killed, wounded, prisoners, and guns captured can never disappear from the account.*

Artillery and prisoners are therefore at all times regarded as the true trophies of victory, as well as its measure, because through these things its extent is declared beyond a doubt. Even the degree of moral superiority may be better judged of by them than by any other relation, especially if the number of killed and wounded is compared therewith ; and here arises a new power increasing the moral effects.

The lost balance of moral power must not be treated lightly because it has no absolute value, and because it does not of necessity appear in all cases in the amount of the results at the final close ; it may become of such excessive weight as to bring down everything with an irresistible force. On that account it may often become a great aim of the operations.

The moral effect of a victory increases, not merely in proportion to the extent of the forces engaged, but in a progressive ratio—that is to say, not only in extent, but also in its intensity. In a beaten detachment order is easily restored. As a single frozen limb is easily revived by the rest of the body, so the courage of a defeated detachment is easily raised again by the courage of the rest of the Army as soon as it rejoins it. If, therefore, the effects of a small victory are not completely done away with, still they are partly lost to the enemy. This is not the case if the Army itself sustains a great defeat ; then one with the other fall together. A great fire attains quite a different heat from several small ones.

If prisoners and captured guns are those things by which the victory principally gains substance, its true crystallizations, then the plan of the battle should have those things specially in view ; the destruction of the enemy by death and wounds appears here merely as a means to an end.

From this arises, in the whole conduct of the War, and especially in great and small combats, a perfect instinct to secure our own line of retreat and to seize that of the enemy ; this follows from the conception of victory, which, as we have seen, is something beyond mere slaughter.

In this effort we see, therefore, the first immediate purpose in the combat, and one which is quite universal. No combat is imaginable in which this effort, either in its double or single form, does not go hand in hand with the plain and simple stroke of force. Even the smallest troop will not throw itself upon its enemy without thinking of its line of retreat, and, in most cases, it will have an eye upon that of the enemy also.

If we now take a look at the conception of victory as a whole, we find in it three elements :

1. The greater loss of the enemy in physical power.

2. In moral power.

3. His open avowal of this by the relinquishment of his intentions.

The returns made up on each side of losses in killed and wounded, are never exact, seldom truthful, and in most cases, full of intentional misrepresentations. Even the statement of the number of trophies is seldom to be quite depended on ; consequently, when it is not considerable it may also cast a doubt even on the reality of the victory. Of the loss in moral forces there is no reliable measure, except in the trophies : therefore, in many cases, the giving up the contest is the only real evidence of the victory. It is this part alone which acts upon the public opinion outside the Army, upon the people and the Government in both belligerent States, and upon all others in any way concerned.

For Generals and Armies whose reputation is not made, this is in itself one of the difficulties in many operations, justified by circumstances when a succession of combats, each ending in retreat, may appear as a succession of defeats, without being so in reality, and when that appearance may exercise a very depressing influence. It is impossible for the retreating General by making known his real intentions to prevent the moral effect spreading to the public and his troops, for to do that with effect he must disclose his plans completely, which of course would run counter to his principal interests to too great a degree.

In order to draw attention to the special importance of this conception of victory we shall only refer to the battle of Soor,[1] the trophies from which were not important (a few thousand prisoners and twenty guns), where Frederick proclaimed his victory by remaining for five days after on the field of battle, although his retreat into Silesia had been previously determined on, and was a measure natural to his whole situation. According to his own account, he thought he would hasten a peace by the moral effect of his victory. Now although a couple of other successes were likewise required, namely, the battle at Katholisch Hennersdorf, in Lusatia, and the battle of Kesseldorf, before this peace took place, still we cannot say that the moral effect of the battle of Soor was *nil*.

If it is chiefly the moral force which is shaken by defeat, and if the number of trophies reaped by the enemy mounts up to an unusual height, then the lost combat becomes a rout, but this is not the necessary consequence of every victory. A rout only sets in when the moral force of the defeated is very severely shaken then there often ensues a complete incapability of further resistance, and the whole action consists of giving way, that is of flight.

ON THE SIGNIFICANCE OF THE COMBAT

As War is nothing but a mutual process of destruction, then the most natural answer in conception, and perhaps also in reality, appears to be that all the powers of each party unite in one great volume and all results in one great shock of these masses. There is certainly much truth in this idea, and it seems to be very advisable that we should adhere to it and should on that account look upon small combats at first only as necessary

[1] Soor, or Sohr, Sept. 30, 1745: Hennersdorf Nov. 23, 1745 ; Kesseldorf, Dec. 15, 1745, all in the Second Silesian War.

loss, like the shavings from a carpenter's plane. Still, however, the thing cannot be settled so easily.

Destruction of the enemy's military forces is in reality the object of all combats ; but other objects may be joined thereto, and these other objects may be at the same time predominant ; we must therefore draw a distinction between those in which the destruction of the enemy's forces is the principal object, and those in which it is more the means. The destruction of the enemy's force, the possession of a place or the possession of some object may be the general motive for a combat, and it may be either one of these alone or several together, in which case however usually one is the principal motive. Now the two principal forms of War, the offensive and defensive, of which we shall shortly speak, do not modify the first of these motives, but they certainly do modify the other two, and therefore if we arrange them in a scheme they would appear thus :

OFFENSIVE	DEFENSIVE
1. Destruction of enemy's force.	1. Destruction of enemy's force.
2. Conquest of a place.	2. Defence of a place.
3. Conquest of some object.	3. Defence of some object.

These motives, however, do not seem to embrace completely the whole of the subject. Strictly speaking, in reconnaissances in which we wish the enemy to show himself, in alarms by which we wish to wear him out, in demonstrations by which we wish to prevent his leaving some point or to draw him off to another, the objects are all such as can only be attained indirectly and *under the pretext of one of the three objects specified in the table,* usually of the second ; for the enemy whose aim is to reconnoitre must draw up his force as if he really intended to attack and defeat us, or drive us off, etc., etc. But this pretended object is not the real one, and our present question is only as to the latter ; therefore, we must to the above three objects of the offensive further add a fourth, which is to lead the enemy to make a false conclusion. That offensive means only are conceivable in connection with this object, lies in the nature of the thing.

On the other hand we must observe that the defence of a place may be of two kinds, either absolute, if as a general question the point is not to be given up, or relative if it is only required for a certain time. The latter happens perpetually in the combats of advanced posts and rear guards.

Here we have a few general observations to make, first, that the importance of the object decreases nearly in the order as they stand above, therefore, that the first of these objects must always predominate in the great battle ; lastly, that the two last in a defensive battle are in reality such as yield no fruit, they are, that is to say, purely negative, and can, therefore, only be serviceable, indirectly, by facilitating something else which is positive. *It is, therefore, a bad sign of the strategic situation if battles of this kind become too frequent.*

DURATION OF THE COMBAT

If we consider the combat no longer in itself but in relation to the other forces of War, then its duration acquires a special importance.

This duration is to be regarded to a certain extent as a second subordinate success. For the conqueror the combat can never be finished too quickly, for the vanquished it can never last too long. A speedy victory indicates a higher power of victory, a tardy decision is, on the side of the defeated, some compensation for the loss.

This is in general true, but it acquires a practical importance in its application to those combats, the object of which is a relative defence.

Here the whole success often lies in the mere duration. This is the reason why we have included it amongst the strategic elements.

The duration of a combat is necessarily bound up with its essential relations. These relations are, absolute magnitude of force, relation of force and (of the different) arms mutually, and nature of the country. Twenty thousand men do not wear themselves out upon one another as quickly as two thousand · we cannot resist an enemy double or three times our strength as long as one of the same strength ; a cavalry combat is decided sooner than an infantry combat ; and a combat between infantry only, quicker than if there is artillery [1] as well ; in

---

[1] The increase in the relative range of artillery and the introduction of shrapnel has altogether modified this conclusion.

hills and forests we cannot advance as quickly as on a level country ; all this is clear enough.

From this it follows, therefore, that strength, relation of the three arms, and position, must be considered if the combat is to fulfil an object by its duration ; but to set up this rule was of less importance to us in our present considerations than to connect with it at once the chief results which experience gives us on the subject.

Even the resistance of an ordinary Division of 8000 to 10,000 men of all arms when opposed to an enemy considerably superior in numbers, will last several hours, if the advantages of country are not too preponderating, and if the enemy is only a little, or not at all, superior in numbers the combat will last half a day. A Corps of three or four Divisions will prolong it to double the time ; an Army of 80,000 or 100,000 to three or four times. Therefore the masses may be left to themselves for that length of time, and no separate combat takes place if within that time other forces can be brought up, whose co-operation mingles then at once into one stream with the results of the combat which has taken place.

These calculations are the result of experience ; but it is important to us at the same time to characterize more particularly the moment of the decision, and consequently the termination.

DECISION OF THE COMBAT

No battle is decided in a single moment, although in every battle there arise moments of crisis, on which the result depends. The loss of a battle is, therefore, a gradual falling of the scale. But there is in every combat a point of time when it may be regarded as decided, in such a way that the renewal of the fight would be a new battle, not a continuation of the old one. To have a clear notion on this point of time, is very important, in order to be able to decide whether, with the prompt assistance of reinforcements, the combat can again be resumed with advantage.

Often in combats which are beyond restoration new forces are sacrificed in vain ; often through neglect the decision has not been seized when it might easily have been secured. Here are two examples which could not be more to the point :

When the Prince of Hohenlohe, in 1806, at Jena, with 35,000 men opposed to from 60,000 to 70,000 under Napoleon, had accepted battle, and lost it—but lost it in such a way that the 35,000 might be regarded as dissolved—General Rüchel undertook to renew the fight with about 12,000 ; the consequence was that in a moment his force was scattered in like manner.

On the other hand, on the same day at Auerstadt, the Prussians maintained a combat with 25,000 against Davoust, who had 28,000, until mid-day ;—but they neglected to use the reserve of 18,000, under General Kalkreuth, to restore the battle which, under these circumstances, it would have been impossible to lose.

Each combat is a whole in which the partial combats combine themselves into one total result. In this total result lies the decision of the combat.

We therefore ask : Which is commonly the moment of the decision, that is to say, that moment when a fresh, effective, of course not disproportionate, force, can no longer turn a disadvantageous battle ?

If we pass over false attacks, which in accordance with their nature are properly without decision, then :

1. If the possession of a movable object was the object of the combat, the loss of the same is always the decision.

2. If the possession of ground was the object of the combat, then the decision generally lies in its loss.

3. But in all other cases, when these two circumstances have not already decided the combat, therefore, particularly in case the destruction of the enemy's force is the principal object, the decision is reached at that moment when the conqueror ceases to feel himself in a state of disintegration, that is, of unserviceableness to a certain extent.

A battle, therefore, in which the assailant has not lost his condition of order and perfect efficiency at all, or, at least, only in a small part of his force, while the opposing forces are, more or less, disorganized throughout, is also not to be retrieved ; and just as little if the enemy has recovered his efficiency.

The smaller, therefore, that part of a force is which has really been engaged, the greater that portion which as reserve has contributed to the result only by its presence, so much the less will any new force of the enemy wrest again the victory from

our hands, and that Commander who carries out to the furthest
with his Army the principle of conducting the combat with the
greatest economy of forces, and making the most of the moral
effect of strong reserves, goes the surest way to victory. Further,
the moment when the crisis-stage of the combat ceases with the
conqueror, and his original state of order is restored, takes place
sooner the smaller the unit he controls.

Again, this moment comes later if night overtakes the conqueror in the crisis, and, lastly, it comes later still if the country
is broken and thickly wooded.

Hitherto, we have considered assistance arriving for the losing
side as a mere increase of force, therefore, as a reinforcement
coming up directly from the rear, which is the most usual case.
But the case is quite different if these fresh forces come upon
the enemy in flank or rear.

By directing a force against the enemy's flank and rear its
efficacy may be much intensified ; but this is so far from being
a necessary result always that the efficacy may, on the other
hand, be just as much weakened.   The circumstances under
which the combat has taken place decide upon this part of the
plan as well as upon every other.   But, at the same time, there
are in it two things of importance for our subject : first, *flank
and rear attacks have, as a rule, a more favourable effect on the
consequences of the decision than upon the decision itself.*   Now as
concerns the retrieving a battle, the first thing to be arrived at
above all is a favourable decision and not magnitude of success.
In this view one would therefore think that a force which comes
to re-establish our combat is of less assistance if it falls upon the
enemy in flank and rear, therefore separated from us, than if it
joins itself to us directly ; certainly, cases are not wanting where
it is so, but we must say that the majority are on the other side,
and they are so on account of the second point which is here
important to us.

This second point *is the moral effect of the surprise, which, as a
rule, a reinforcement coming up to re-establish a combat has generally
in its favour.*   Who does not feel that an attack in flank or rear,
which at the commencement of the battle, when the forces are
concentrated and prepared for such an event would be of little
importance, gains quite another weight in the last moment
of the combat !

We must, therefore, at once admit that in most cases a re-inforcement coming up on the flank or rear of the enemy will be more efficacious. Here results almost defy calculation, because the moral forces gain completely the ascendancy. This is, therefore, the right field for boldness and daring.

If the combat is to be regarded as not yet ended, then the new contest which is opened by the arrival of assistance fuses into the former. But this is not the case if the combat was already decided ; then there are two results separate from each other. Now if the assistance which arrives is not in itself alone a match for the enemy, then a favourable result is hardly to be expected from this second combat : but if it is so strong that it can undertake the second combat without regard to the first, then it may be able by a favourable issue to compensate or even over-balance the first combat.

But when a battle proceeding disadvantageously is arrested and turned before its conclusion, its minus result on our side not only disappears from the account, but also becomes the foundation of a greater victory. If now the total result turns in our favour, if we wrest from the enemy the field of battle and recover all the trophies again, then all the forces which he has sacrificed in obtaining them become sheer gain for us, and our former defeat becomes a stepping-stone to a greater triumph. Such is the alteration which the magic of victory and the curse of defeat produces in the specific weight of the same elements.

Therefore, even if we are decidedly superior in strength, and are able to repay the enemy his victory by a greater still, it is always better to forestall the conclusion of a disadvantageous combat, if it is of proportionate importance, so as to turn its course rather than to deliver a second battle.

We have still another conclusion to examine.

If in a regular pitched battle, the decision has gone against one, this does not constitute a motive for determining on a new one. The determination for this new one must proceed from other relations. This conclusion, however, is opposed by a moral force. From the oldest Field-Marshal to the youngest drummer-boy troops are never in better spirits for fighting than when they have to wipe out a stain. This is, however, only on the supposition that the beaten portion is not too great in proportion to the whole, because otherwise the above feeling is lost in that of powerlessness.

There is therefore a very natural tendency to use this moral force to repair the disaster on the spot. It then lies in the nature of the case that this second battle must be an offensive one.

In the catalogue of battles of second-rate importance there are many examples to be found of such retaliatory battles ; but great battles have generally too many other determining causes to be brought on by this weaker motive.

THE BATTLE

ITS DECISION

What is a battle ? A conflict of the main body, but not an unimportant one about a secondary object, not a mere attempt which is given up when we see betimes that our object is hardly within our reach : it is a conflict waged with all our forces for the attainment of a decisive victory.

Minor objects may also be mixed up with the principal object, and it will take many different tones of colour from the circumstances out of which it originates, for a battle belongs also to a greater whole of which it is only a part. Its distinguishing character is, that unlike all other encounters, it is arranged for, and undertaken with the sole purpose of obtaining a decisive victory.

This has an influence on the *manner of its decision*, on the *effect of the victory contained in it,* and determines *the value which theory is to assign to it as a means to an end.* On that account we make it the subject of our special consideration.

If a battle takes place principally on its own account, the elements of its decision must be contained in itself ; in other words, victory must be striven for as long as a possibility or hope remains. It must not, therefore, be given up on account of secondary circumstances.

Now how is that precise moment to be described ?

If a certain artificial formation and cohesion of an Army is the principal condition under which the bravery of the troops can gain a victory, *then the breaking up of this formation* is the decision. A beaten wing which is put out of joint decides the fate of all that was connected with it. If the essence of the defence consists in an intimate alliance of the Army with the ground on which it fights and its obstacles, so that Army and position are only one, then the *conquest* of *an essential point* in this position is the decision.

According to our conception of it, the order of battle is only a disposition of the forces suitable to the convenient use of them, and the course of the battle a mutual slow wearing away of these forces upon one another, to see which will have soonest exhausted his adversary.

The resolution therefore to give up the fight arises, in a battle more than in any other combat, from the relation of the fresh reserves remaining available ; for only these still retain all their moral vigour, and the cinders of the battered, knocked-about battalions, already burnt out in the destroying element, must not be placed on a level with them ; also lost ground as we have elsewhere said, is a standard of lost moral force ; it therefore comes also into account, but more as a sign of loss suffered than for the loss itself, and the number of fresh reserves is always the chief point to be looked at by both Commanders.

The result of the whole combat consists in the sum total of the results of all partial combats ; but these results of separate combats are settled by different considerations.

First by the pure moral power in the mind of the leading officers. If a General of Division has seen his battalions forced to succumb, it will have an influence on his demeanour and his reports, and these again will have an influence on the measures of the Commander-in-Chief. Secondly, by the quicker melting away of our troops, which can be easily estimated. Thirdly, by lost ground. All these things serve for the eye of the General as a compass to tell the course of the battle in which he is embarked.

We have already said more than once that the final decision is ruled mostly by the relative number of the fresh reserves remaining at the last ; that Commander who sees that his adversary is decidedly superior to him in this respect makes up his mind to retreat. So long as that Commander against whom the issue seems to declare itself still retains a superiority in reserve force, he will not give up the day. But from the moment that his reserves begin to become weaker than his enemy's, the decision may be regarded as settled, and what he now does depends partly on special circumstances, partly on the degree of courage and perseverance which he personally possesses, and which may degenerate into foolish obstinacy. How a Commander can attain to the power of estimating correctly the still remaining reserves on both sides is an affair of skilful practical genius. The resolution requires some special immediate causes. Of these there are two chief ones which constantly recur, that is, the danger of retreat, and the arrival of night.

If the retreat with every new step which the battle takes in its course becomes constantly in greater danger, and if the reserves are so much diminished that they are no longer adequate to get breathing room, then there is nothing left but to submit to fate.

But night as a rule puts an end to all battles, because a night combat holds out no hope of advantage except under particular circumstances ; and as night is better suited for a retreat than the day, so, therefore, the Commander who must look at the retreat as a thing inevitable, or as most probable, will prefer to make use of the night for his purpose.

That there are, besides the above two usual and chief causes, yet many others also, which are less or more individual and not to be overlooked, is a matter of course.

As a conclusion to this subject, we must dwell for a moment on the point at which the courage of the Commander engages in a sort of conflict with his reason.

If, on the one hand the overbearing pride of a victorious conqueror, if the inflexible will of a naturally obstinate spirit, if the strenuous resistance of noble feelings will not yield the battlefield, where they must leave their honour, yet on the other hand, reason counsels not to give up everything, not to risk the last upon the game, but to retain as much over as is necessary for an orderly retreat. However highly we must esteem courage and firmness in War, and however little prospect there is of victory to him who cannot resolve to seek it by the exertion of all his power, still there is a point beyond which perseverance can only be termed desperate folly, and therefore can meet with no approbation from any critic. In the most celebrated of all battles, that of Waterloo, Napoleon used his last rserve in an effort to retrieve a battle which was past being retrieved. He spent his last farthing, and then, as a beggar, abandoned both the battlefield and his crown.

EFFECTS OF VICTORY

According to the point from which our view is taken, we may feel as much astonished at the extraordinary results of some great battles as at the want of results in others. We shall dwell for a moment on the nature of the effect of a great victory.

Three things may easily be distinguished here : the effect upon the instrument itself, that is, upon the Generals and their Armies ; the effect upon the States interested in the War ; and the particular result of these effects as manifested in the subsequent course of the campaign.

If we only think of the trifling difference which there usually is between victor and vanquished in killed, wounded, prisoners, and artillery lost on the field of battle itself, the consequences which are developed out of this insignificant point seem often quite incomprehensible, and yet, usually, everything only happens quite naturally.

We have already said that the magnitude of a victory increases not merely in the same measure as the vanquished forces increase in number, but in a higher ratio. The moral effects resulting from the issue of a great battle are greater on the side of the conquered than on that of the conqueror. On this moral effect we must therefore lay special weight. Its chief effect is upon the vanquished, because here it is the direct cause of fresh losses, and besides it is homogeneous in nature with danger, with the fatigues, the hardships, and generally with all those embarrassing circumstances by which War is surrounded, therefore enters into league with them and increases by their help, whilst with the conqueror all these things are like weights which give a higher swing to his courage. It is therefore found, that the vanquished sinks much further below the original line of equilibrium than the conqueror raises himself above it ; on this account, if we speak of the effects of victory we allude more particularly to those which manifest themselves in the vanquished army.

Again, the moral effect of victory in our battles is greater than

it was in the earlier ones of modern military history. If the
former are as we have depicted them, a real struggle of forces
to the utmost, then the sum total of all these forces, of the
physical as well as the moral, must decide more than certain
special dispositions or mere chance.

A single fault committed may be repaired next time ; from
good fortune and chance we can hope for more favour on
another occasion ; but the sum total of moral and physical
powers cannot be so quickly altered, and, therefore, what the
award of a victory has decided appears of much greater importance for all futurity.

He who has not been present at the loss of a great battle will
have difficulty in forming for himself a living or quite true idea
of it, and the abstract notions of this or that small untoward
affair will never come up to the perfect conception of a lost
battle. Let us stop a moment at the picture.

The first thing which overpowers the imagination—and we
may indeed say, also the understanding—is the diminution
of the masses ; then the loss of ground, which takes place always,
more or less, and, therefore, on the side of the assailant also, if
he is not fortunate ; then the rupture of the original formation,
the jumbling together of troops, the risks of retreat, which, with
few exceptions may always be seen sometimes in a less, sometimes
in a greater degree ; next the retreat, the most part of which
commences at night, or, at least, goes on throughout the night.
On this first march we must at once leave behind a number of
men completely worn out and scattered about, often just the
bravest, who have been foremost in the fight who held out the
longest : the feeling of being conquered, which only seized
the superior officers on the battlefield, now spreads through
all ranks, even down to the common soldiers, aggravated by
the horrible idea of being obliged to leave in the enemy's hands
so many brave comrades, who but a moment since were of
such value to us in the battle, and aggravated by a rising distrust
of the chief Commander, to whom, more or less, every subordinate attributes as a fault the fruitless efforts he has made ;
and this feeling of being conquered is no ideal picture over
which one might become master ; it is an evident truth that
the enemy is superior to us ; a truth of which the causes might
have been so latent before that they were not to be discovered,

but which, in the issue, comes out clear and palpable, or which was also, perhaps, before suspected, but which in the want of any certainty, we had to oppose by the hope of chance, reliance on good fortune, Providence or a bold attitude. Now, all this has proved insufficient, and the bitter truth meets us harsh and imperious.

It is evident that an Army in this condition, looked at as an instrument, is weakened ! How can we expect that when reduced to such a degree that, as we said before, it finds new enemies in all the ordinary difficulties of making War, it will be able to recover by fresh efforts what has been lost ! Before the battle there was a real or assumed equilibrium between the two sides ; this is lost, and, therefore, some external assistance is requisite to restore it ; every new effort without such external support can only lead to fresh losses.

Thus, therefore, the most moderate victory of the chief Army must tend to cause a constant sinking of the scale on the opponent's side, until new external circumstances bring about a change. If these are not near, if the conqueror is an eager opponent, who, thirsting for glory, pursues great aims, then a first-rate Commander, and in the beaten Army a true military spirit, hardened by many campaigns are required, in order to stop the swollen stream of prosperity from bursting all bounds, and to moderate its course by small but reiterated acts of resistance, until the force of victory has spent itself at the goal of its career.

And now the effect of defeat beyond the Army, upon the Nation and Government ! It is the sudden collapse of hopes stretched to the utmost, the downfall of all self-reliance. In place of these extinct forces, fear, with its destructive properties of expansion, rushes into the vacuum left, and completes the prostration.

The consequences which the effect of victory brings forth in the course of the War itself depend in part on the character and talent of the victorious General, but more on the circumstances from which the victory proceeds, and to which it leads. Without boldness and an enterprising spirit on the part of the leader, the most brilliant victory will lead to no great success.

But then the question may be asked, Can theory accept this effect of victory as absolutely necessary ?—must it not rather

endeavour to find out counteracting means capable of neutral-
izing these effects ? It seems quite natural to answer this question
in the affirmative ; but heaven defend us from taking that wrong
course of most theories, out of which is begotten a mutually
devouring *Pro et Contra*.

Certainly that effect is perfectly necessary, for it has its foundation in the nature of things, and it exists, even if we find means
to struggle against it.

STRATEGIC MEANS OF UTILIZING VICTORY

The pursuit of a beaten Army commences at the moment
that Army, giving up the combat, leaves its position ; all
previous movements in one direction and another belong not
to that but to the progress of the battle itself. Usually victory
at the moment here described, even if it is certain, is still as yet
small and weak in its proportions, and would not rank as an
event of any great positive advantage if not completed by a
pursuit on the first day. Then it is mostly, as we have before
said, that the trophies which give substance to the victory begin
to be gathered up. Of this pursuit we shall speak in the next
place.

Usually both sides come into action with their physical powers
considerably deteriorated, for the movements immediately
preceding have generally the character of very urgent circumstances. The efforts which the forging out of a great combat
costs, complete the exhaustion ; from this it follows that the
victorious party is very little less disorganized and out of his
original formation than the vanquished, and therefore requires
time to reform, to collect stragglers, and issue fresh ammunition
to those who are without. All these things place the conqueror
himself in the state of crisis of which we have already spoken.
If now the defeated force is only a detached portion of the
enemy's Army, or if it has otherwise to expect a considerable
reinforcement, then the conqueror may easily run into the
obvious danger of having to pay dear for his victory. Even
when a strong accession of force by the enemy is not to be
feared, the conqueror finds in the above circumstances a powerful check to the vivacity of his pursuit. Morevoer, at this
moment the whole weight of all that is sensuous in an Army,

its wants and weaknesses, are dependent on the will of the Commander. All the thousands under his command require rest and refreshment, and long to see a stop put to toil and danger for the present. He himself, through mental and bodily fatigue, is more or less weakened in his natural activity, and thus it happens then that, mostly from these causes, purely incidental to human nature, less is done than might have been done. It is only thus we can explain the hesitating manner in which many Generals follow up a victory which superior numbers have given them.

The first pursuit of the enemy we limit in general to the extent of the first day, including the night following the victory. At the end of that period the necessity of rest for ourselves prescribes a halt in any case.

This first pursuit has different natural degrees. It amounts usually more to alarming and watching than to pressing the enemy in reality, because the smallest obstacle of ground is generally sufficient to check the pursuit.

The second degree is the pursuit made by a strong advance-guard composed of all arms. Such a pursuit generally drives the enemy as far as the nearest strong position for his rear-guard, or the next position affording space for his Army. Neither can usually be found at once, and, therefore, the pursuit can be carried further ; generally, however, it does not extend beyond the distance of one or at most a couple of leagues, because otherwise the advance-guard would not feel itself sufficiently supported.

The third and most vigorous degree is when the victorious Army itself continues to advance as far as its physical powers can endure. In this case the beaten Army will generally quit such ordinary positions as a country usually offers on the mere show of an attack, or of an intention to turn its flank ; and the rear-guard will be still less likely to engage in an obstinate resistance.

As a rule, night puts an end to pursuit, even when the battle has only been decided shortly before darkness sets in. This allows the conquered either time for rest and to rally immediately, or, if he retreats during the night it gives him a march in advance. After this break the conquered is decidedly in a better condition ; much of that which had been thrown into confusion has been brought again into order, ammunition has been renewed, the whole has been put into a fresh formation. Whatever further encounter now takes place with the enemy is a new battle not a continuation of the old, and although it may be far from promising absolute success, still it is a fresh combat, and not merely a gathering up of the *debris* by the victor.

When, therefore, the conqueror can continue the pursuit istelf throughout the night, if only with a strong advance-guard composed of all arms of the service, the effect of the victory is immensely increased.

The deduction is, that the energy thrown into the pursuit chiefly determines the value of the victory ; that this pursuit is a second act of the victory, in many cases more important also than the first, and that strategy, whilst here approaching tactics to receive from it the harvest of success, exercises the first act of her authority by demanding this completion of the victory.

But further, the effects of victory are very seldom found to stop with this first pursuit ; now first begins the real career to which victory lent velocity.

In the further stages of pursuit, again, we can distinguish three degrees : the simple pursuit, a hard pursuit, and a parallel march to intercept.

The simple *following* or *pursuing* causes the enemy to continue his retreat, until he thinks he can risk another battle. It will therefore in its effect suffice to exhaust the advantages gained, and besides that, all that the enemy cannot carry with him, sick, wounded, and disabled from fatigue, quantities of baggage, and carriages of all kinds, will fall into our hands, but this mere following does not tend to heighten the disorder in the enemy's Army, an effect which is produced by the two following causes.

If, for instance, instead of contenting ourselves with taking up every day the camp the enemy has just vacated, occupying just as much of the country as he chooses to abandon, we make our arrangements so as every day to encroach further, and accordingly with our advance-guard organized for the purpose, attack his rear-guard every time it attempts to halt, then such a course will hasten his retreat, and consequently tend to increase his disorganization.—This it will principally effect by the character of continuous flight, which his reateat will thus assume. Nothing has such a depressing influence on the soldier, as the sound of the enemy's cannon afresh at the moment when, after a forced march he seeks some rest ; if this excitement is continued from day to day for some time, it may lead to a complete rout. There lies in it a constant admission of being obliged to obey the law of the enemy, and of being unfit for any resistance, and the consciousness of this cannot do otherwise than weaken the morale of an Army in a high degree. The effect of pressing the enemy in this way attains a maximum when it drives the enemy to make night marches. If the conqueror scares away the discomfited opponent at sunset from a camp which has just been taken up either for the main body of the Army, or for the rear-guard, the conquered must either make a night march, or alter his position in the night, retiring further away, which is much the same thing ; the victorious party can on the other hand pass the night in quiet.

The arrangement of marches, and the choice of positions depend in this case also upon many other things, especially on the supply of the Army, on strong natural obstacles in the country, on large towns, etc., etc. But nevertheless it is true and practicable that marches in pursuit may be so planned as to compel the enemy to march at night while we take our rest, and that the efficacy of the pursuit is very much enhanced thereby.

Lastly, the third and most effectual form of pursuit is, the *parallel march* to the immediate object of the retreat.

Every defeated Army will naturally have behind it, at a greater or less distance, some point, the attainment of which is the first purpose in view, whether it be that failing in this its further retreat might be compromised, as in the case of a defile, or that it is imporant for the point itself to reach it before the enemy, as in the case of a great city, magazines, etc., or, lastly, that the Army at this point will gain new powers of defense, such as a strong position, or junction with other corps.

Now if the conqueror directs his march on this point by a lateral road, it is evident how that may quicken the retreat of the beaten Army in a destructive manner, convert it into hurry, perhaps into flight. The conquered has only three ways to counteract this : the first is to throw himself in front of the enemy; this plainly supposes an enterprising bold General, and an excellent Army, beaten but not utterly defeated.

The second way is hastening the retreat; but this is just what the conqueror wants, and it easily leads to immoderate efforts on the part of the troops, by which enormous losses are sustained, in stragglers, broken guns, and carriages of all kinds.

The third way is to make a *detour*, and get round the nearest point of interception, to march with more ease at a greater distance from the enemy, and thus to render the haste required less damaging. This last way is the worst of all, it generally turns out like a new debt contracted by an insolvent debtor. There are cases in which this course is advisable; others where there is nothing else left; also instances in which it has been successful; but upon the whole it is certainly true that its adoption is usually influenced less by a clear persuasion of its being the surest way of attaining the aim than the dread of encountering the enemy. Woe to the Commander who gives in to this! However much the moral of his Army may have deteriorated, and however well founded may be his apprehensions of being at a disadvantage in any conflict with the enemy, the evil will only be made worse by too anxiously avoiding every possible risk of collision. Napoleon in 1813 would never have brought over the Rhine with him the 30,000 or 40,000 men who remained after the battle of Hanau, if he had avoided that battle and tried to pass the Rhine at Mannheim or Coblenz. It is just by means of small combats carefully prepared and executed, that the moral strength of the Army can first be resuscitated.

The beneficial effect of the smallest successes is incredible; but with most Generals the adoption of this plan implies great self-command. The other way, that of evading all encounter, appears so much easier.

We must, however, recollect here that we are speaking of a whole Army, not of a single Division, which, having been cut off, is seeking to join the main Army by making a *detour*; in such a case circumstances are different, and success is not uncommon.

Such marches tell upon the pursuer as well as the pursued, and they are not advisable if the enemy's Army rallies itself upon another considerable one; if it has a distinguished General at its head, and if its destruction is not already well prepared. But when this means can be adopted, it acts also like a great mechanical power. The losses of the beaten Army from sickness and fatigue are on such a disproportionate scale, the spirit of the Army is so weakened and lowered by the constant solicitude about impending ruin, that at last anything like a well-organized stand is out of the question ; every day thousands of prisoners fall into the enemy's hands without striking a blow. In such a season of complete good fortune, the conquerer need not hesitate about dividing his forces in order to draw into the vortex of destruction everything within reach of his Army, to cut off detachments, to take fortresses unprepared for defense, to occupy large towns, etc., etc. He may do anything until a new state of things arises, and the more he ventures in this way the longer will it be before that change will take place.

RETREAT AFTER A LOST BATTLE

In a lost battle the power of an Army is broken, the moral to a greater degree than the physical. A second battle unless fresh favourable circumstances come into play, would lead to a complete defeat, perhaps, to destruction. This is a military axiom. According to the usual course the retreat is continued up to that point where the equilibrium of forces is restored, either by reinforcements, or by the protection of strong fortresses, or by great defensive positions afforded by the country, or by a separation of the enemy's force. The magnitude of the losses sustained, the extent of the defeat, but still more the character of the enemy, will bring nearer or put off the instant of this equilibrium. How many instances may be found of a beaten Army rallied again at a short distance, without its circumstances having altered in any way since the battle. The cause of this may be traced to the moral weakness of the adversary, or to the preponderance gained in the battle not having been sufficient to make a lasting impression.

To profit by this weakness or mistake of the enemy, not to yield one inch breadth more than the pressure of circumstances demands, but above all things, in order to keep up the moral forces to as advantageous a point as possible, a slow retreat, offering incessant resistance, and bold courageous counterstrokes, whenever the enemy seeks to gain any excessive advantages, are absolutely necessary. Retreats of great Generals and of Armies inured to War have always resembled the retreat of a wounded lion, and such is, undoubtedly, also the best theory.

It is true that at the moment of quitting a dangerous position we have often seen trifling formalities observed which caused a waste of time, and were, therefore, attended with danger, whilst in such cases everything depends on getting out of the place speedily. Practised Generals reckon this maxim a very important one. But such cases must not be confounded with a general retreat after a lost battle. Whoever then thinks by a few rapid marches to gain a start, and more easily to recover a firm standing commits a great error. The first movements should be as small as possible, and it is a maxim in general not to suffer ourselves to be dictated to by the enemy. This maxim cannot be followed without bloody fighting with the enemy at our heels, but the gain is worth the sacrifice.

A strong rear-guard composed of picked troops, commanded by the bravest General, and supported by the whole Army at critical moments, a careful utilization of ground, strong ambuscades wherever the boldness of the enemy's advance-guard, and the ground, afford opportunity ; in short, the preparation and the system of regular small battles,—these are the means of following this principle.

Now and again it has been suggested to retreat in separate divisions or even eccentrically. Such a separation as is made merely for convenience, and along with which concentrated action continues possible and is kept in view, is not what we now refer to ; any other kind is extremely dangerous.

IV

OFFENCE AND DEFENCE

CONCEPTION OF DEFENCE

WHAT IS DEFENCE IN CONCEPTION ? THE WARDING OFF A BLOW. What is then its characteristic sign ? The state of expectancy (or of waiting for this blow). By this sign alone can the defensive be distinguished from the offensive in War. But an absolute defence completely contradicts the idea of War, because there would then be War carried on by one side only. It follows that the defence in War can only be relative and the above distinguishing signs must therefore only be applied to the essential idea or general conception : it does not apply to all the separate acts which compose the War.

But as we must return the enemy's blows if we are really to carry on War on our side, therefore this offensive act in defensive War takes place more or less under the general title defensive. We can, therefore, in a defensive campaign fight offensively, in a defensive battle we may use some Divisions for offensive purposes, and lastly, while remaining in position awaiting the enemy's onslaught, we still make use of the offensive by sending at the same time bullets into the enemy's ranks. The defensive form in War is therefore no mere shield but a shield formed of blows delivered with skill.

What is the object of defence ? *To preserve.* To preserve is easier than to acquire ; from which follows at once that the means on both sides being supposed equal, the defensive is easier than the offensive. But in what consists the greater facility of preserving ? In this, that all time not turned to any account falls into the scale in favour of the defence. Every suspension of offensive action, either from erroneous views, from fear or from indolence, is in favour of the side acting defensively.

Having established these general ideas we now turn more directly to the subject. As the defensive has a negative object, *preserving,* and the offensive a positive object, *conquering,* and as the latter increases our own means of carrying on War, but the preserving does not, therefore in order to express ourselves distinctly, we must say, *that the defensive form of War is in itself stronger than the offensive.*

If the defensive is the stronger form of conducting War, but has a negative object, it follows of itself that we must only use it so long as our weakness compels us to, and that we must give up that form as soon as we feel strong enough to aim at the positive object. Now as the state of our circumstances is usually improved in the event of our gaining a victory through the assistance of the defensive, it is therefore, also, the natural course in War to begin with the defensive, and to end with the offensive. It is therefore in contradiction with the conception of War to suppose the defensive the ultimate object of the War. A war in which victories are merely used to ward off blows, and where there is no attempt to return the blow, would be just as absurd as a battle in which the most absolute defence (passivity) should everywhere prevail.

If the offensive form was the stronger every one would be for attacking, and the defensive would be an absurdity. If we look to experience, such a thing is unheard of as any one carrying on a War upon two different theatres—offensively on one with the weaker Army, and defensively on the other with his strongest force. But if the reverse of this has everywhere and at all times taken place, it shows plainly that Generals, although their own inclination prompts them to the offensive, still hold the defensive to be the stronger form.

THE OFFENSIVE AND DEFENSIVE IN TACTICS

We must inquire into the circumstances which give the victory in a battle.

Superiority of numbers, and bravery, discipline as a rule, depend on things which lie out of the province of the Art of War in the sense in which we are now considering it ; but irrespective of these things, there are three which appear of decisive importance in tactics : *surprise, advantage of ground, and the attack from several quarters.* The surprise produces an effect by opposing to the enemy a great many more troops than he expected at some particular point. The superiority in numbers in this case is very different to a general superiority of numbers ; it is the most powerful agent in the Art of War.

The advantage of ground contributes to the victory, scarped grounds, high hills, marshy streams, hedges, inclosures, etc. We also allude to the advantage which ground affords as cover, under which troops are concealed from view. Even from ground apparently featureless a person acquainted with the locality may derive assistance. The attack from several quarters includes all tactical turning movements great and small, and its effects are derived partly from the double execution obtained in this way from firearms, and partly from the enemy's dread of his retreat being cut off.

THE OFFENSIVE AND DEFENSIVE IN STRATEGY

In Strategy, the success is the successful preparation of the tactical victory ; the greater this strategic success, the more probable becomes the victory in the battle. On the other hand, strategic success lies in the making use of the victory gained. The more events the strategic combinations can in the sequel include in the consequences of a battle gained, the more Strategy can lay hands on amongst the wreck of all that has been shaken to the foundation by the battle, the more it sweeps up in great masses what of necessity has been gained with great labour by many single hands in the battle, the grander will be its success. Those things which chiefly lead to this success, or at least facilitate it, are :

1. The advantage of ground.

2. The surprise, either in the form of an actual attack by surprise or by the unexpected display of large forces at certain points.

3. The attack from several quarters (all three, as in tactics).

4. The assistance of the theatre of War by fortresses, and everything belonging to them.

5. The support of the people.

6. The utilization of great moral forces.

Now, what are the relations of offensive and defensive with respect to these things ?

The Defender has the advantage of ground ; the Assailant that of the attack by surprise in Strategy, as in tactics. In tactics, a surprise seldom rises to the level of a great victory, while in Strategy it often finishes the war at one stroke. But at the same time we must observe that the advantageous use of this means supposes some *great* and *uncommon*, as well as *decisive* error committed by the adversary, therefore it does not alter the balance much in favour of the offensive.

Attacks in flank and rear, which in Strategy mean on the sides and reverse of the theatre of War, are of a very different nature to attacks so called in tactics. On account of the greater spaces in Strategy, the enveloping attack, or the attack from several sides, as a rule is only possible for the side which has the initiative, that is the offensive.

The fourth principle, the *Assistance of the Theatre of War*, is naturally an advantage on the side of the defensive. If the attacking Army opens the campaign, it breaks away from its own theatre, and is thus weakened, that is, it leaves fortresses and depots of all kinds behind it. The greater the sphere of operations which must be traversed, the more it will be weakened (by marches and garrisons) ; the Army on the defensive continues to keep up its connection with everything, that is, it enjoys the support of its fortresses, is not weakened in any way, and is near to its sources of supply.

The support of the population as a fifth principle is not realized in every defence, for a defensive campaign may be carried on in the enemy's country, but still this principle is only derived from the idea of the defensive, and applies to it in the majority of cases. Besides, by this is meant chiefly, although not exclusively, the effect of calling out the last reserves.

Napoleon's campaign of 1812, gives as it were in a magnifying glass a very clear illustration of the effect of the means specified under principles 3 and 4. 500,000 men passed the Niemen, 120,000 fought at Borodino, and much fewer arrived at Moscow.

We may say that the effect itself of this stupendous attempt was so disastrous that even if the Russians had not assumed any offensive at all, they would still have been secure from any fresh attempt at invasion for a considerable time. It is true that with the exception of Sweden there is no country in Europe which is situated like Russia, but the efficient principle is always the same, the only distinction being in the greater or less degree of its strength.

If we add to the fourth and fifth principles, the consideration that these forces of the defensive belong to the original defensive, that is the defensive carried on in our own soil, and that they are much weaker if the defence takes place in an enemy's country and is mixed up with an offensive undertaking, then from that there is a new disadvantage for the offensive, much the same as above, in respect to the third principle ; for the offensive is just as little composed entirely of active elements, as the defensive of mere warding off blows ; indeed every attack which does not lead directly to peace must inevitably end in the defensive.

There still remains to be mentioned one small factor, the high spirit, the feeling of superiority in an Army which springs from a consciousness of belonging to the attacking party. The thing is in itself a fact, but the feeling soon merges into the more general and more powerful one imparted by victory or defeat, by the talent or incapacity of the General.

CHARACTER OF STRATEGIC DEFENSIVE

Even if the intention of a War is only the maintenance of the existing situation of things, still a mere parrying of a blow is something quite contradictory to the conception of the term War, because the conduct of War is no mere state of endurance. If the defender has obtained an important advantage, then the defensive form has done its part, and under the protection of this success he must give back the blow, otherwise he exposes himself to certain destruction ; common sense points out that we should use the advantage gained to guard against a second attack. How, when, and where this reaction shall commence is subject to a number of other conditions. We must always consider this transition to an offensive return as a natural tendency of the defensive, and always conclude that there is something wrong in the management of a War when a victory gained through the defensive form is not turned to good account in any manner.

A swift and vigorous assumption of the offensive is the most brilliant point in the defensive ; he who does not from the first include this transition in his idea of the defensive will be forever thinking only of the means which will be consumed by the enemy and gained by ourselves through the offensive, which means, however, depend not on tying the knot, but on untying it. Further, it is a stupid confusion of ideas if, under the term offensive, we always understand sudden attack or surprise, and consequently under defensive imagine nothing but embarrassment and confusion.

It is true that a conqueror makes his determination to go to War sooner than the unconscious defender, and if he knows how to keep his measures properly secret, he may also perhaps take the defender unawares ; but that is a thing quite foreign to War itself, for it should not be so. War actually takes place more for the defensive than for the conqueror, for invasion only calls forth resistance, and it is not until there is resistance that there is War. A conqueror is always a lover of peace (as Napoloen always asserted of himself) ; he would like to make his entry into our State unopposed ; in order to prevent this, we must choose War, and therefore also make preparations. It is just the weak, or that side which must defend itself, which should be always armed in order not to be taken by surprise.

The appearance of one side sooner than the other in the theatre of War depends in most cases on things quite different from a view to offensive or defensive. But although a view to one or other of these forms is not the cause, it is often the result of this priority of appearance. Whoever is first ready will on that account go to work offensively, if the advantage of surprise is sufficient to make it expedient ; and the party who is the last to be ready can only then in some measure compensate for the disadvantage which threatens him by the advantages of the defensive.

If we imagine to ourselves a defensive, such as it should be, we must suppose it with every possible preparation of all means, with an Army fit for, and inured to, War, with a General who does not wait for his adversary with anxiety from an embarrassing feeling of uncertainty, but from his own free choice, with cool presence of mind, with fortresses which do not dread a siege, and lastly, with a loyal people who fear the enemy as little as he fears them. With such attributes the defensive will act no such contemptible part in opposition to the offensive, and the latter will not appear such an easy and certain form of War, as it does in the gloomy imaginations of those who can only see in the offensive courage, strength of will, and energy ; in the defensive, helplessness and apathy.

If in military history we rarely find such great victories resulting from the defensive battle as from the offensive, that proves nothing against our assertion that the one is as well suited to produce victory as the other ; the real cause is in the very different relations of the defender. The Army acting on the defensive is generally the weaker of the two, not only in the amount of his forces, but in every other respect ; he either is, or thinks he is, not in a condition to follow up his victory with great results, and contents himself with merely fending off the danger and saving the honour of his arms. That the defender by inferiority of force and other circumstances may be tied down to that degree we do not dispute, but there is no doubt that this, which is only the consequence of a contingent necessity, has often been assumed to be the consequence of that part which every defender has to play ; and thus in an absurd manner it has become a prevalent view of the defensive that its battles should really be confined to warding off the attacks of the enemy, and not directed to the destruction of the enemy. We hold this to be a prejudicial error, a regular substitution of the form for the thing itself ; and we maintain unreservedly that in the form of War we call *defence*, the victory may not only be more probable, but may also attain the same magnitude and efficacy as in the attack, and that this may be the case not only in the *total result* of all the combats which constitute a campaign, but also in any *particular* battle, if the necessary degree of force and energy is not wanting.

GUERRILLA WARFARE

A people's War in general is to be regarded as a consequence of the outburst which the military element in our day has made through its old formal limits ; as an expansion and strengthening of the whole fermentation-process which we call War. The requisition system, the immense increase in the size of Armies by means of that system, and the general liability to military service, the employment of militia, are all things which lie in the same direction, if we make the limited military system of former days our starting-point ; and the *levée en masse*, or arming of the people, now lies also in the same direction. In the generality of cases, the people who make judicious use of people-Wars, will gain a superiority over those who despise its use. Then the question is whether this intensification of the military element is, upon the whole, salutary for the interests of humanity or otherwise—a question it would be about as easy to answer as the question of War itself—we leave both to philosophers. But the opinion may be advanced, that the resources swallowed up in people's Wars might be more profitably employed in providing other military means ; no very deep investigation is necessary to be convinced that these resources are for the most part not disposable, and cannot be utilized in an arbitrary manner at pleasure. One essential part, that is the moral element, is not called into existence until this kind of employment for it arises.

We therefore do not ask again : how much does the resistance which the whole Nation in Arms is capable of making, cost that Nation ? but we ask : what is the effect which such a resistance can produce ? What are its conditions, and how is it to be used ?

Defensive means widely dispersed, are not suited to great blows requiring concentrated action in time and space. Its operation is according to the surface. The greater that surface and the greater the contact with the enemy's Army, and consequently the more that Army spreads itself out, so much the greater will be the effects of arming the Nation. Like a slow gradual heat, it destroys the foundations of the enemy's Army. As it requires time to produce its effects, therefore whilst the hostile elements are working on each other, there is a state of tension which either gradually wears out if the people's War is extinguished at some points, and burns slowly away at others, or leads to a crisis, if the flames of this general conflagration envelop the enemy's Army, and compel it to evacuate the country to save itself from utter destruction. In order that this result should be produced by a national War alone, we must suppose either a surface-extent of the dominions invaded, exceeding that of any country in Europe, except Russia, or suppose a disproportion between the strength of the invading Army and the extent of the country, such as never occurs in reality. Therefore, to avoid following a phantom, we must imagine a people-War always in combination, with a War carried on by a regular Army, and both carried on according to a plan embracing the operations of the whole.

The conditions under which alone the people's War can become effective are the following :

1. That the War is carried on in the heart of the country.
2. That it cannot be decided by a single catastrophe.
3. That the theatre of War embraces a considerable extent of country.
4. That the national character is favourable to the measure.
5. That the country is of a broken and difficult nature, either from being mountainous, or by reason of woods and marshes, or from the peculiar mode of cultivation in use.

National levies and armed peasantry cannot and should not be employed against the main body of the enemy's Army, or even against any considerable detachment of the same. They must not attempt to crack the nut, they must only gnaw on the surface and the borders. We entertain no exaggerated ideas of the omnipotence of a people's War, such as that it is an inexhaustible, unconquerable element, over which the mere force of an Army has as little control as the human will has over the wind or the rain. Still we must admit that armed peasants are not to be driven before us in the same way as a body of soldiers who keep together like a herd of cattle. Armed peasants, when broken, disperse in all directions, for which no formal plan is required ; through this circumstance, the march of every small body of troops in a mountainous, thickly wooded, or even broken country, becomes very dangerous, for at any moment a combat may arise ; if no armed bodies have even been seen for some time, the same peasants already driven off by the head of a column may at any hour make their appearance in its rear.

A people's War should never condense into a solid body. Still, it should collect at some points into denser masses, and form threatening clouds from which now and again a formidable flash of lightning may burst forth.

The easiest way for a General to produce this form of a national armament, is to support the movement by small detachments sent from the Army. But this has its limits ; partly, first, because it would be detrimental to the Army to cut it up into detachments, to dissolve it into a body of irregulars ; secondly, partly because experience seems to tell us that when there are too many regular troops in a district, the people's War loses in vigour and efficacy ; the causes of this are in the first place, that too many of the enemy's troops are thus drawn into the district, and, in the second place, that the inhabitants then rely on their own regular troops, and, thirdly, because the presence of such large bodies of troops makes too great demands on the powers of the people in other ways, that is, in providing quarters, transport, contributions, etc., etc.

In the defensive combat a persistent slow systematic action is required, and great risks must be run ; a mere attempt, from which we can desist as soon as we please, can never lead to results in the defensive. If, therefore, the national levies are entrusted with the defence of any particular portion of territory, care must be taken that the measure does not lead to a regular great defensive combat ; for if the cirumstances were ever so favourable to them, they would be sure to be defeated. They should, therefore, defend the approaches to mountains, dykes, over marshes, river-passages, as long as possible ; but when once they are broken, they should rather disperse, and continue their defense by sudden attacks, than concentrate and allow themselves to be shut up in some narrow last refuge in a regular defensive position. However brave a nation may be, however warlike its habits, however intense its hatred of the enemy, however favourable the nature of the country, it is an undeniable fact that a people's War cannot be kept up in an atmosphere too full of danger.

No State should believe its fate, its entire existence, to be dependent upon one battle, even the most decisive. If it is beaten, the calling forth fresh power, and the natural weakening which every offensive undergoes with time, may bring about a turn of fortune, or assistance may come from abroad. No such urgent haste to die is needed yet ; in the natural course of the moral world a people should try the last means of deliverance when it sees itself hurried along to the brink of an abyss.

However small and weak a State may be in comparison to its enemy, if it foregoes a last supreme effort, we must say there is no longer any soul left in it. This does not exclude the possibility of saving itself from complete destruction by the purchase of peace at a sacrifice ; but neither does such an aim on its part do away with the utility of fresh measures for defence ; they will neither make peace more difficult nor more onerous, but easier and better. They are still more necessary if there is an expectation of assistance from those who are interested in maintaining our political existence. Any Government, therefore, which, after the loss of a great battle, only thinks how it may speedily place the Nation in the lap of peace, and unmanned by the feeling of great hopes disappointed, no longer feels in itself the courage or the desire to stimulate to the utmost every element of force, completely stultifies itself in such case through weakness, and shows itself unworthy of victory, and, perhaps, just on that account, was incapable of gaining one.

ENDS IN WAR MORE PRECISELY DEFINED

The aim of War in conception must always be the overthrow of the enemy ; this is the fundamental idea from which we set out.

Now, what is this overthrow ? It does not always imply as necessary the complete conquest of the enemy's country. According to the majority of ascertained facts, the following circumstances chiefly bring about the overthrow of the enemy :

(1) Dispersion of his Army if it forms, in some degree, a potential force.

(2) Capture of the enemy's capital city, if it is both the centre of the power of the State and the seat of political assemblies and factions.

(3) An effectual blow against the principal Ally, if he is more powerful than the enemy himself.

We have always hitherto supposed the enemy in War as a unity, which is allowable for considerations of a very general nature. But having said that the subjugation of the enemy lies in the overcoming his resistance, concentrated in the centre of gravity, we must lay aside this supposition and introduce the case in which we have to deal with more than one opponent.

If two or more States combine against a third, that combination constitutes, in a political aspect, only *one* War, at the same time this political union has also its degrees.

The question is whether each State in the coalition possesses an independent interest in, and an independent force with which to prosecute, the War ; or whether there is one amongst them on whose interests and forces those of the others lean for support. The more that the last is the case, the easier it is to look upon the different enemies as one alone, and the more readily we can simplify our principal enterprise to one great blow ; and as long as this is in any way possible, it is the most thorough and complete means of success.

We may, therefore, establish it as a principle, that if we can conquer all our enemies by conquering one of them, the defeat of that one must be the aim of the War, because in that one we hit the common centre of gravity of the whole War.

An operation in War, like everything else upon earth, requires its time ; but there is no trace to be found in War of any reciprocal action between time and force, such as takes place in dynamics.

Time is necessary to both belligerents, and the only question is : Which of the two, judging by his position, has most reason to expect *special advantages* from time ? Now (exclusive of peculiarities in the situation on one side or the other) the *vanquished* has plainly the most reason. Envy, jealousy, anxiety for self, as well as now and again magnanimity, are the natural intercessors for the unfortunate ; they raise up for him on the one hand friends, and on the other hand weaken and dissolve the coalition amongst his enemies. Therefore, by delay something advantageous is more likely to happen for the conquered than for the conqueror.

But if the conquered provinces are sufficiently important, if there are in them points which are essential to the well-being of those parts which are not conquered, so that the evil, like a cancer, is perpetually of itself gnawing further into the system, then it is possible that the conqueror, although nothing further is done, may gain more than he loses. Now in this state of circumstances, if no help comes from without, then time may complete the work thus commenced ; what still remains unconquered will, perhaps, fall of itself.

Our object in the above reasoning has been to show clearly that no conquest can be finished too soon, that spreading it over a *greater space of time* than is absolutely necessary for its completion, instead of *facilitating* it, makes it more *difficult*.

We have said that, under the expression "overthrow of the enemy," we understand the real absolute aim of the "act of War"; now we shall see what remains to be done when the conditions under which this object might be attained do not exist.

These conditions presuppose a great physical or moral superiority, or a great spirit of enterprise, an innate propensity to extreme hazards. Now where all this is not forthcoming, the aim in the act of War can only be of two kinds; either the conquest of some small or moderate portion of the enemy's country, or the defense of our own until better times; this last is the usual case in defensive War.

Whether the one or the other of these aims is of the right kind can always be settled by calling to mind the expression used in reference to the last. *The waiting till more favourable times* implies that we have reason to expect such times hereafter, and this waiting for, that is, defensive War, is always based on this prospect; on the other hand, offensive War, that is, the taking advantage of the present moment, is always to be commended when the future holds out a better prospect, not to ourselves, but to our adversary.

The third case, which is probably the most common, is when neither party has anything definite to look for from the future. In this case the offensive War is plainly imperative upon him who is politically the aggressor, that is, who has the positive motive.

We have here decided for offensive or defensive War on grounds which have nothing to do with the relative forces of the combatants respectively, and yet it may appear that it would be nearer right to make the choice of the offensive or defensive chiefly dependent on the mutual relations of combatants in point of military strength; our opinion is, that in doing so we should just leave the right road.

Let us suppose a small State which is involved in a contest with a very superior power, and foresees that with each year its position will become worse: should it not, if War is inevitavle, make use of the time when its situation is furthest from the worst? Then it must attack, not because the attack *in itself* ensures any advantages—it will rather increase the disparity of forces—but because this State is under the necessity of either

bringing the matter completely to an issue before the worst
time arrives, or of gaining at least in the meantime some advantages which it may hereafter turn to account. This theory
cannot appear absurd. But if this small State is quite certain
that the enemy will advance against it, then, certainly, it can
and may make use of the defensive against its enemy to procure
a first advantage ; there is then at any rate no danger of losing
time.

V

PLAN OF WAR

THE PLAN OF THE WAR COMPREHENDS THE WHOLE MILITARY Act; through it that Act becomes a whole, which must have one final determinate object, in which all particular objects must become absorbed. No War is commenced, or, at least, no War should be commenced, without first seeking a reply to the question: What is to be attained by and in the same? The first is the final object; the other is the intermediate aim. By this chief consideration the whole course of the War is prescribed, the extent of the means and the measure of energy are determined; its influence manifests itself down to the smallest organ of action.

INTERDEPENDENCE OF THE PARTS IN WAR

In the absolute form of war, where everything is the effect of its natural and necessary cause, one thing follows another in rapid succession; there is, if we may use the expression, no neutral space; there is—on account of the manifold reactionary effects which War contains in itself, on account of the connection in which, strictly speaking, the whole series of combats follow one after another, on account of the culminating point which every victory has, beyond which losses and defeats commence—on account of all these natural relations of War there is, I say, only *one result*, to wit, the *final result*. Until it takes place nothing is decided, nothing won, nothing lost. Here we may say indeed: the end crowns the work. In this view, therefore, War is an indivisible whole, the parts of which (the subordinate results) have no value except in their relation to this whole.

To this view of the relative connection of results in War, which may be regarded as extreme, stands opposed another extreme, according to which War is composed of single independent results, in which, as in any number of games played,

the preceding has no influence on the next following ; everything here, therefore, depends only on the sum total of the
results, and we can lay up each single one like a counter
at play.

Just as the first kind of view derives its truth from the nature
of things, so we find that of the second in history. There are
cases without number in which a small moderate advantage
might have been gained without any very onerous condition
being attached to it. The more the element of War is modified
the more common these cases become.

If we keep to the first of these supposed views, we must
perceive the necessity of every War being looked upon as a
whole from the very commencement, and that at the very first
step forward, the Commander should have in his eye the object
to which every line must converge.

If we admit the second view, then subordinate advantages
may be pursued on their own account, and the rest left to
subsequent events.

As neither of these forms of conception is entirely without
result, therefore theory cannot dispense with either. But it
makes this difference in the use of them, that it requires the first
to be laid as a fundamental idea at the root of everything, and
that the latter shall only be used as a modification which is
justified by circumstances.

OF THE MAGNITUDE OF THE OBJECT OF THE WAR AND THE EFFORTS TO BE MADE

The compulsion which we must use towards our enemy
will be regulated by the proportions of our own and his political
demands. In so far as these are mutually known they will give
the measure of the mutual efforts ; but they are not always
quite so evident, and this may be a first ground of a difference
in the means adopted by each.

The situation and relations of the States are not like each
other ; this may become a second cause.

The strength of will, the character and capabilities of the
Governments are as little like ; this is a third cause.

These three elements cause an uncertainty in the calculation
of the amount of resistance to be expected, consequently an

uncertainty as to the amount of means to be applied and the object to be chosen.

In order to ascertain the real scale of the means which we must put forth for War, we must think over the political object both on our own side and on the enemy's side ; we must consider the power and position of the enemy's State as well as of our own, the character of his Government and of his people, and the capacities of both, and all that again on our own side, and the political connections of other States, and the effect which the War will produce on those States. That the determination of these diverse circumstances and their diverse connections with each other is an immense problem, that it is the true flash of genius which discovers here in a moment what is right, and that it would be quite out of the question to become master of the complexity merely by a methodical study, it is easy to conceive. In this sense Napoleon was quite right when he said that it would be a problem in algebra before which a Newton might stand aghast.

First of all, therefore, we must admit that the judgment on an approaching War, on the end to which it should be directed and on the means which are required, can only be formed after a full consideration of the whole of the circumstances in connection with it : with which therefore must also be combined the most individual traits of the moment ; next, that this decision, like all in military life, cannot be purely objective, but must be determined by the mental and moral qualities of Princes, Statesmen, and Generals, whether they are united in the person of one man or not. We must allow ourselves here a passing glance at history.

Half-civilized Tartars, the republics of ancient times, the feudal lords and commercial cities of the Middle Ages, kings of the eighteenth century, and, lastly, princes and people of the nineteenth century, all carry on War in their own way, carry it on differently, with different means, and for a different object.

The Tartars seek new abodes. They march out as a nation with their wives and children, they are, therefore, greater than any other Army in point of numbers, and their object is to make the enemy submit or expel him altogether.

The old republics, with the exception of Rome, were of

small extent ; still smaller their Armies, for they excluded the great mass of the populace ; therefore their Wars were confined to devastating the open country and taking some towns in order to ensure to themselves in these a certain degree of influence for the future.

Rome alone forms an exception, but not until the later period of its history. It was only after having spread itself by means of alliances all over Southern Italy, that it began to advance as a really conquering power.

Just as peculiar in their way are the Wars of Alexander. With a small Army, but distinguished for its intrinsic perfection, he overthrew the decayed fabric of the Asiatic States ; without rest, and regardless of risks, he traversed the breadth of Asia, and penetrated into India. No republics could do this. Only a King, in a certain measure his own condottiere, could get through so much so quickly.

The great and small monarchies of the Middle Ages carried on their Wars with feudal levies. The feudal force itself was raised through an organization of vassaldom ; the bond which held it together was partly legal obligation, partly a voluntary contract ; the whole formed a real confederation. The armament and tactics were based on the right of might. All this influenced the character of the Wars at that period in the most distinct manner. They were comparatively rapidly carried out, there was little time spent idly in camps, but the object was generally only punishing, not subduing the enemy.

The great commercial towns and small republics brought forward the condottieri. That was an expensive, and therefore, as far as visible strength, a very limited military force ; as for its intensive strength, it was of still less value in that respect ; so far from their showing anything like extreme energy or impetuosity in the field, their combats were generally only sham-fights.

The feudal system condensed itself by degrees into a decided territorial supremacy ; the feudal levies were turned into mercenaries. The condottieri formed the connecting-link in the change, and were therfore for a time, the instrument of the more powerful States ; but this had not lasted long when the soldier, hired for a limited term, was turned into a *standing mercenary*, and the military force of States now became an Army, having its base in the public treasury.

The relations of the States of Europe at these periods were quite as peculiar as their military forces. Upon the whole this part of the world had split up into a mass of petty States. A State could not be considered as a real unity ; it was rather an agglomeration of loosely connected forces. It is from this point of view we must look at the foreign politics and Wars of the Middle Ages.

The end of the seventeenth century, the time of Louis XIV, is to be regarded as the point in history at which the standing military power, such as it existed in the eighteenth century, reached the zenith. Through rapid strides in social improvements, and a more enlightened system of government, France had become very great in comparison to what it had been.

The other relations of States had likewise altered. Europe was divided into a dozen kingdoms and two republics. Internal relations had almost everywhere settled down into a pure monarchical form.

At this epoch appeared three new Alexanders—Gustavus Adolphus, Charles XII, and Frederick the Great, whose aim was, by small but highly disciplined Armies, to raise little States to the rank of great monarchies, and to throw down everything that opposed them.

But what War gained on the one side in force and consistency was lost again on the other side.

Armies were supported out of the treasury, which the Sovereign regarded partly as his private purse. Relations with other States, except with respect to a few commercial subjects, mostly concerned only the interests of the treasury or of the Government, not those of the people. The people, therefore, were in the eighteenth century absolutely nothing directly, having only still an indirect influence on the War, through their virtues and faults.

In this manner, in proportion as the Government separated itself from the people, and regarded itself as the State, War became more exclusively a business of the Government. The consequence of this was, that the means which the Government could command had tolerably well-defined limits, which could be mutually estimated, both as to their extent and duration ; this robbed War of its most dangerous feature. War became a regular game in which Time and Chance shuffled the cards ; but in its signification it was only diplomacy somewhat intensified, a more vigorous way of negotiating, in which battles and sieges were substituted for diplomatic notes. The Army, with its fortresses and some prepared positions, constituted a State in a State, within which the element of War slowly consumed itself. All Europe rejoiced at its taking this direction, and held it to be the necessary consequence of the spirit of progress. Although there lay in this an error, inasmuch as the progress of the human mind can never lead to what is absurd, still upon the whole this change had a beneficial effect for the people.

Thus matters stood when the French Revolution broke out ; Austria and Prussia tried their diplomatic Art of War ; this very soon proved insufficient. War had again suddenly become an affair of the people, and that of a people numbering thirty millions, every one of whom regarded himself as a citizen of the State. By this participation of the people in the War instead of a Cabinet and an Army, a whole Nation with its natural weight came into the scale. Henceforward, the means available—the efforts which might be called forth—had no longer any definite limits ; the energy with which the War itself might be conducted had no longer any counterpoise, and consequently the danger for the adversary had risen to the extreme.

If the whole War of the Revolution passed over without all this making itself felt in its full force and becoming quite evident, the cause lay in that technical incompleteness with which the French had to contend, which showed itself first amongst the common soldiers, then in the Generals, lastly, at the time of the Directory, in the Government itself.

After all this was perfected by the hand of Napoleon, this military power, based on the strength of the whole nation, marched over Europe, smashing everything in pieces so surely and certainly, that where it only encountered the old-fashioned Armies the result was not doubtful for a moment. A reaction, however, awoke in due time. In Spain, the War became of itself an affair of the people. In Austria, in the year 1809, the

Government commenced extraordinary efforts, by means of Reserves and Landwehr, which were nearer to the true object, and far surpassed in degree what this State had hitherto conceived possible. In Russia, in 1812, the example of Spain and Austria was taken as a pattern, the enormous dimensions of that Empire on the one hand allowed the preparations, although too long deferred, still to produce effect ; and, on the other hand, intensified the effect produced. The result was brilliant. In Germany, Prussia rose up the first, made the War a National Cause, and without either money or credit and with a population reduced one-half, took the field with an Army twice as strong as that of 1806.

Therefore, since the time of Napoleon, War, through being first on one side, then again on the other, an affair of the whole Nation, has assumed quite a new nature, or rather it has approached much nearer to its real nature, to its absolute perfection. The means then called forth had no visible limit, the limit losing itself in the energy and enthusiasm of the Government and its subjects. By the extent of the means and the wide field of possible results, as well as by the powerful excitement of feeling which prevailed, energy in the conduct of War was immensely increased ; the object of its action was the downfall of the foe ; and not until the enemy lay powerless on the ground was it supposed to be possible to stop or to come to any understanding with respect to the mutual objects of the contest.

Thus, therefore, the element of War, freed from all conventional restrictions, broke loose, with all its natural force. The cause was the participation of the people in this great *affair of State*, and this participation arose partly from the effects of the French Revolution on the internal affairs of countries, partly from the threatening attitude of the French towards all Nations.

Now, whether this will be the case always in future, whether all Wars hereafter in Europe will be carried on with the whole power of the States, and, consequently, will only take place on account of great interests closely affecting the people, or whether a separation of the interests of the Government from those of the people will again gradually arise, would be a difficult point to settle ; least of all shall we take it upon ourselves to settle it. But every one will agree with us, that bounds, which to a certain extent existed only in an unconsciousness of what is possible, when once thrown down, are not easily built up again ; and that, at least, whenever great interests are in dispute, mutual hostility will discharge itself in the same manner as it has done in our times.

VI

WAR AND POLITICS

WE NEVER FIND THAT A STATE JOINING IN THE CAUSE OF another State takes it up with the same earnestness as its own. An auxiliary Army of moderate strength is sent ; if it is not successful, then the Ally looks upon the affair as in a manner ended, and tries to get out of it on the cheapest terms possible.

The thing would have a kind of consistency, and it would be less embarrassing to the theory of War if this promised contingent was handed over entirely to the State engaged in War, so that it could be used as required ; it might then be regarded as a subsidised force. But the usual practice is widely different. Generally the auxilliary force has its own Commander, who depends only on his own Government, and to whom it prescribes an object such as best suits the shilly-shally measures it has in view.

But even if two States go to War with a third, they do not always both look in like measure upon this common enemy as one that they must destroy or be destroyed by themselves.

Lastly, even in Wars carried on without Allies, the political cause of a War has a great influence on the method in which it is conducted.

If we only require from the enemy a small sacrifice, then we content ourselves with aiming at a small equivalent by the War, and we expect to attain that by moderate efforts. The enemy reasons in very much the same way. Now, if one or the other finds that he has erred in his reckoning—that in place of being slightly superior to the enemy, as he supposed, he is, if anything, rather weaker, still, at that moment, money and all other means, as well as sufficient moral impulse for greater exertions, are very often deficient : in such a case he just does what is called " the best he can ; " hopes better things in the future, although he has not the slightest foundation for such hope, and the War in the meantime drags itself feebly along, like a body worn out with sickness.

That the theory of War, if it is to be and to continue a philosophical study, finds itself here in a difficulty is clear. All that is essentially inherent in the conception of War seems to fly from it, and it is in danger of being left without any point of support. But the natural outlet soon shows itself. According as a modifying principle gains influence over the act of War, or rather, the weaker the motives to action become, the more the action will glide into a passive resistance, the less eventful it will become, and the less it will require guiding principles. All military art then changes itself into mere prudence, the principal object of which will be to prevent the trembling balance from suddenly turning to our disadvantage, and the half War from changing into a complete one.

Having made the requisite examination on both sides of that state of antagonism in which the nature of War stands with relation to other interests of men individually and of the bond of society, in order not to neglect any of the opposing elements—an antagonism which is founded in our own nature, and which, therefore, no philosophy can unravel—we shall now look for that unity into which, in practical life, these antagonistic elements combine themselves by partly neutralising each other. We should have brought forward this unity at the very commencement if it had not been necessary to bring out this contradiction very plainly, and also to look at the different elements separately. Now, this unity is *the conception that War is only a part of political intercourse, therefore by no means an independent thing in itself.*

We know, certainly, that War is only called forth through the political intercourse of Governments and Nations ; but in general it is supposed that such intercourse is broken off by War, and that a totally different state of things ensues, subject to no laws but its own.

We maintain, on the contrary, that War is nothing but a continuation of political intercourse, with a mixture of other means. We say mixed with other means in order thereby to maintain at the same time that this political intercourse does not cease by the War itself, is not changed into something quite different, but that, in its essence, it continues to exist, whatever may be the form of the means which it uses, and that the chief lines on which the events of the War progress, and to which they are attached, are only the general features of policy which run all through the War until peace takes place. And how can we conceive it to be otherwise? Does the cessation of diplomatic notes stop the political relations between different Nations and Governments? Is not War merely another kind of writing and language for political thoughts? It has certainly a grammar of its own, but its logic is not peculiar to itself.

Accordingly, War can never be separated from political intercourse, and if, in the consideration of the matter, this is done in any way, all the threads of the different relations are, to a certain extent, broken, and we have before us a senseless thing without an object.

This kind of idea would be indispensable even if War was perfect War, the perfectly unbridled element of hostility, for all the circumstances on which it rests, the enemy's power. Allies on both sides, the characteristics of the people and their Governments respectively, etc.,—are they not of a political nature, and are they not so intimately connected with the whole political intercourse that it is impossible to separate them?

If War belongs to policy, it will naturally take its character from thence. The only question is whether in framing plans for a War the political point of view should give way to the purely military (if such a point is conceivable), that is to say, should disappear altogether, or subordinate itself to it, or whether the political is to remain the ruling point of view and the military to be considered subordinate to it.

If we reflect on the nature of real War, and call to mind that War is to be regarded as an organic whole, from which the single branches are not to be separated, then it becomes certain and palpable to us that the superior standpoint for the conduct of the War, from which its leading lines must proceed, can be no other than that of policy.

In one word, the Art of War in its highest point of view is policy, but, no doubt, a policy which fights battles instead of writing notes.

According to this view, to leave a great military enterprise, or the plan for one, to a *purely military judgment and decision* is a distinction which cannot be allowed, and is even prejudicial.

This is perfectly natural. None of the principal plans which are required for a War can be made without an insight into the political relations ; and, in reality, when people speak, as they often do, of the prejudicial influence of policy on the conduct of a War, they say in reality something very different to what they intend. It is not this influence but the policy itself which should be found fault with. *If policy is right then it can only act with advantage on the War. If this influence of policy causes a divergence from the object, the cause is only to be looked for in a mistaken policy.*

These errors first displayed themselves in the Napoleonic Wars, and the events of these Wars completely disappointed the expectations which policy entertained. But this did not take place because policy neglected to consult its military advisers. That Art of War in which the politician of the day could believe, namely, that derived from the reality of War at that time, that which belonged to the policy of the day, that familiar instrument which policy had hitherto used—*that* Art of War, I say, was naturally involved in the error of policy, and therefore could not teach it anything better. It is true that War itself underwent important alterations both in its nature and forms, which brought it nearer to its absolute form ; but these changes were not brought about because the French Government had, to a certain extent, delivered itself from the leading-strings of policy ; they arose from an altered policy, produced by the French Revolution, not only in France, but over the rest of Europe as well. This policy had called forth other means and other powers, by which it became possible to conduct War with a degree of energy which could not have been thought of otherwise.

Thus, the actual changes in the Art of War, too, are a consequence of alterations in policy ; and, so far from being an argument for the possible separation of the two, they are, on the contrary, very strong evidence of the intimacy of their connection.

Therefore, once more : War is an instrument of policy ; it must necessarily bear its character, it must measure with its scale : the conduct of War, in its great features, is therefore policy itself, which takes up the sword in place of the pen, but does not on that account cease to think according to its own laws.

VII

CONCLUSIONS

Definition

WAR IS NOTHING BUT A DUEL ON AN EXTENSIVE SCALE. IF WE would conceive as a unit the countless number of duels which make up a War, we shall do so best by supposing to ourselves two wrestlers. Each strives by physical force to compel the other to submit to his will : each endeavours to throw his adversary, and thus render him incapable of further resistance.

War therefore is an act of violence intended to compel our opponent to fulfil our will.

Violence arms itself with the inventions of Art and Science in order to contend against violence. Self-imposed restrictions, almost imperceptible and hardly worth mentioning, termed usages of International Law, accompany it without essentially impairing its power. Violence, that is to say, physical force (for there is no moral force without the conception of States and Law), is therefore the *means* ; the compulsory submission of the enemy to our will is the ultimate *object*. In order to attain this object fully, the enemy must be disarmed, and disarmament becomes therefore the immediate object of hostilities in theory. It takes the place of the final object, and puts it aside as something we can eliminate from our calculations.

Utmost Use of Force

Now, philanthropists may easily imagine there is a skilful method of disarming and overcoming an enemy without causing great bloodshed, and that this is the proper tendency of the Art of War. However plausible this may appear, still it is an error which must be extirpated ; for in such dangerous things as War, the errors which proceed from a spirit of benevolence are the worst. As the use of physical power to the utmost extent by no means excludes the co-operation of the intelligence, it follows that he who uses force unsparingly, without reference to the bloodshed involved, must obtain a superiority if his adversary uses less vigour in its application. The former then dictates the law to the latter, and both proceed to extremities to which the only limitations are those imposed by the amount of counteracting force on each side.

This is the way in which the matter must be viewed, and it is to no purpose, it is even against one's own interest, to turn away from the consideration of the real nature of the affair because the horror of its elements excites repugnance.

If the Wars of civilized people are less cruel and destructive than those of savages, the difference arises from the social condition both of States in themselves and in their relations to each other. Out of this social condition and its relations War arises, and by it War is subjected to conditions, is controlled and modified. But these things do not belong to War itself; they are only given conditions; and to introduce into the philosophy of War itself a principle of moderation would be an absurdity.

Two motives lead men to War: instinctive hostility and hostile intention. In our definition of War, we have chosen as its characteristic the latter of these elements, because it is the most general. It is impossible to conceive the passion of hatred of the wildest description, bordering on mere instinct, without combining with it the idea of a hostile intention. On the other hand, hostile intentions may often exist without being accompanied by any, or at all events by any extreme, hostility of feeling. Amongst savages views emanating from the feelings, amongst civilized nations those emanating from the understanding, have the predominance; but this difference arises from attendant circumstances, existing institutions, etc., and, therefore, is not to be found necessarily in all cases, although it prevails in the majority. In short, even the most civilized nations may burn with passionate hatred of each other.

We may see from this what a fallacy it would be to refer the War of a civilized nation entirely to an intelligent act on the part of the Government, and to imagine it as continually freeing itself more and more from all feeling of passion in such a way that at last the physical masses of combatants would no longer be required; in reality, their mere relations would suffice—a kind of algebraic action.

If War is an *act* of force, it belongs necessarily also to the feelings. If it does not originate in the feelings, it *reacts*, more or less, upon them, and the extent of this reaction depends not on the degree of civilization, but upon the importance and duration of the interests involved.

Therefore, if we find civilized nations do not put their prisoners to death, do not devastate towns and countries, this is because their intelligence exercises greater influence on their mode of carrying on War, and has taught them more effectual means of applying force than these rude acts of mere instinct. The invention of gunpowder, the constant progress of improvements in the construction of firearms, are sufficient proofs that the tendency to destroy the adversary which lies at the bottom of the conception of War is in no way changed or modified through the progress of civilization.

We therefore repeat our proposition, that War is an act of violence pushed to its utmost bounds; as one side dictates the law to the other, there arises a sort of reciprocal action, which logically must lead to an extreme. This is the first reciprocal action, and the first extreme with which we meet (*first reciprocal action*).

The Aim is to Disarm the Enemy

We have already said that the aim of all action in War is to disarm the enemy, and we shall now show that this, theoretically ar least, is indispensable.

If our opponent is to be made to comply with our will, we must place him in a situation which is more oppressive to him than the sacrifice which we demand; but the disadvantages of this position must naturally not be of a transitory nature, at least in appearance, otherwise the enemy, instead of yielding, will hold out, in the prospect of a change for the better. Every change in this position which is produced by a continuation of the War should therefore be a change for the worse. The worst condition in which a belligerent can be placed is that of being completely disarmed. If, therefore, the enemy is to be reduced to submission by an act of War, he must either be positively disarmed or placed in such a position that he is threatened with it. From this it follows that the disarming or overthrow of the enemy, whichever we call it, must always be the aim of Warfare. Now War is always the shock of two hostile bodies in collision, not the action of a living power upon an inanimate mass, because an absolute state of endurance would not be making War ; therefore, what we have just said as to the aim of action in War applies to both parties. Here, then, is another case of reciprocal action. As long as the enemy is not defeated, he may defeat me ; then I shall be no longer my own master ; he will dictate the law to me as I did to him. This is the second reciprocal action, and leads to a second extreme (*second reciprocal action*).

Utmost Exertion of Powers

If we desire to defeat the enemy, we must proportion our efforts to his powers of resistance. This is expressed by the product of two factors which cannot be separated, namely, *the sum of available means* and *the strength of the Will*. The sum of the available means may be estimated in a measure, as it depends (although not entirely) upon numbers ; but the strength of volition is more difficult to determine, and can only be estimated to a certain extent by the strength of the motives. Granted we have obtained in this way an approximation to the strength of the power to be contended with, we can then take a review of our own means, and either increase them so as to obtain a preponderance, or, in case we have not the resources to effect this, then do our best by increasing our means as far as possible. But the adversary does the same ; therefore, there is a new mutual enhancement, which, in pure conception, must create a fresh effort towards an extreme. This is the third case of reciprocal action, and a third extreme with which we meet (*third reciprocal action*).

Modification in the Reality

Thus reasoning in the abstract, the mind cannot stop short of an extreme, because it has to deal with an extreme, with a conflict of forces left to themselves, and obeying no other but their own inner laws.

But everything takes a different shape when we pass from abstractions to reality. In the former, everything must be subject to optimism, and we must imagine the one side as well as the other striving after perfection and even attaining it. Will this ever take place in reality ? It will if,

(1) War becomes a completely isolated act, which arises suddenly, and is in no way connected with the previous history of the combatant States.

(2) If it is limited to a single decision, or to several simultaneous decisions.

(3) If it contains within itself the solution perfect and complete, and if the political situation which will follow from it does not affect its conduct.

War is never an Isolated Act

With regard to the first point, neither of the two opponents is an abstract person to the other, not even as regards that factor in the sum of resistance which does not depend on objective things, viz., the Will. This Will is not an entirely unknown quantity ; it indicates what it will be to-morrow by what it is to-day. War does not spring up quite suddenly, it does not spread to the full in a moment ; each of the two opponents can, therefore, form an opinion of the other, in a great measure, from what he is and what he does, instead of judging of him according to what he, strictly speaking, should be or should do.

War does not Consist of a Single Instantaneous Blow

The second point gives rise to the following considerations :

If War ended in a single decision, or a number of simultaneous ones, then naturally all the preparations for the same would have a tendency to the extreme, for an omission could not in any way be repaired ; the utmost, then, that the world of reality could furnish as a guide for us would be the preparations of the enemy, as far as they are known to us. But if the result is made up from several successive acts, then naturally that which precedes with all its phases may be taken as a measure for that which will follow.

Yet every War would necessarily resolve itself into a single solution, or a sum of simultaneous results, if all the means required for the struggle were raised at once, or could be at once raised.

But we have already seen that even in the preparation for War the real world steps into the place of mere abstract conception, and therefore all forces are not at once brought forward.

It lies also in the nature of these forces and their application that they cannot all be brought into activity at the same time. These forces are the *armies actually on foot, the country,* with its superficial extent and its population, *and the allies.*

In point of fact, the country, with its superficial area and the population, besides being the source of all military force, constitutes in itself an integral part of the efficient quantities in War, providing either the theatre of war or exercising a considerable influence on the same.

Now, it is possible to bring all the movable military forces of a country into operation at once, but not all fortresses, rivers, mountains, people, etc.—in short, not the whole country, unless it is so small that it may be completely embraced by the first act of the War. Further, the co-operation of allies does not depend on the Will of the belligerents ; and from the nature of the political relations of states to each other, this co-operation is frequently not afforded until after the War has commenced, or it may be increased to restore the balance of power.

That this part of the means of resistance, which cannot at once be brought into activity, in many cases, is a much greater part of the whole than might at first be supposed, and that it often restores the balance of power, will be more fully shown hereafter. Here it is sufficient to show that a complete concentration of all available means in a moment of time is contradictory to the nature of War.

Now, this in itself, furnishes no ground for relaxing our efforts to accumulate strength to gain the first result, because an unfavourable issue is always a disadvantage to which no one would purposely expose himself, and also because the first decision, although not the only one, still will have the more influence on subsequent events, the greater it is in itself.

But the possibility of gaining a later result causes men to take refuge in that expectation, owing to the repugnance in the human mind to making excessive efforts ; and therefore forces are not concentrated and measures are not taken for the first decision with that energy which would otherwise be used. Whatever one belligerent omits from weakness, becomes to the other a real objective ground for limiting his own efforts, and thus again, through this reciprocal action, extreme tendencies are brought down to efforts on a limited scale.

The Result in War is never Absolute

Lastly, even the final decision of a whole War is not always to be regarded as absolute. The conquered State often sees in it only a passing evil, which may be repaired in after times by means of political combinations. How much this must modify the degree of tension, and the vigour of the efforts made, is evident in itself.

The Probabilities of Real Life take the Place of the Conceptions of the Extreme and the Absolute

In this manner, the whole act of War is removed from the rigorous law of forces exerted to the utmost. If the extreme is no longer to be apprehended, and no longer to be sought for, it is left to the judgment to determine the limits for the efforts to be made in place of it, and this can only be done on the data furnished by the facts of the real world by the *laws of probability*. Once the belligerents are no longer mere conceptions, but individual States and Governments, once the War is no longer an ideal, but a definite substantial procedure, then the reality will furnish the data to compute the unknown quantities which are required to be found.

From the character, the measures, the situation of the adversary, and the relations with which he is surrounded, each side will draw conclusions by the law of probability as to the designs of the other, and act accordingly.

The Political Object now Reappears

Here the question which he had laid aside forces itself again into consideration, viz., *the political object of the War.* The law of the extreme, the view to disarm the adversary, to overthrow him, has hitherto to a certain extent usurped the place of this end or object. Just as this law loses its force, the political object must again come forward. If the whole consideration is a calculation of probability based on definite persons and relations, then the political object, being the original motive, must be an essential factor in the product. The smaller the sacrifice we demand from our opponent, the smaller, it may be expected, will be the means of resistance which he will employ ; but the smaller his preparation, the smaller will ours require to be. Further, the smaller our political object, the less value shall we set upon it, and the more easily shall we be induced to give it up altogether.

Thus, therefore, the political object, as the original motive of the War, will be the standard for determining both the aim of the military force and also the amount of effort to be made. This it cannot be in itself, but it is so in relation to both the belligerent States, because we are concerned with realities, not with mere abstractions. One and the same political object may produce totally different effects upon different people, or even upon the same people at different times ; we can, therefore, only admit the political object as the measure, by considering it in its effects upon those masses which it is to move, and consequently the nature of those masses also comes into consideration. It is easy to see that thus the result may be very different according as these masses are animated with a spirit which will infuse vigour into the action or otherwise. It is quite possible for such a state of feeling to exist between two States that a very trifling political motive for War may produce an effect quite disproportionate—in fact, a perfect explosion.

This applies to the efforts which the political object will call forth in the two States, and to the aim which the military action shall prescribe for itself. At times it may itself be that aim, as, for example, the conquest of a province. At other times the political object itself is not suitable for the aim of military action ; then such a one must be chosen as will be an equivalent for it, and stand in its place as regards the conclusion of peace. But also, in this, due attention to the peculiar character of the States concerned is always supposed. There are circumstances in which the equivalent must be much greater than the political object, in order to secure the latter. The political object will be so much the more the standard of aim and effort, and have more influence in itself, the more the masses are indifferent, the less that any mutual feeling of hostility prevails in the two States from other causes, and therefore there are cases where the political object almost alone will be decisive.

If the aim of the military action is an equivalent for the political object, that action will in general diminish as the political object diminishes, and in a greater degree the more the political object dominates. Thus it is explained how, without any contradiction in itself, there may be Wars of all degrees of importance and energy, from a War of extermination down to the mere use of an army of observation. This, however, leads to a question of another kind which we have hereafter to develop and answer.

A Suspension in the Action of War Unexplained by Anything said as Yet

However insignificant the political claims mutually advanced, however small the aim to which military action is directed, can this action be suspended even for a moment ? This is a question which penetrates deeply into the nature of the subject.

Every transaction requires for its accomplishment a certain time we call its duration. This may be longer or shorter, according as the person acting throws more or less dispatch into his movements.

About this more or less we shall not trouble ourselves here. Each person acts in his own fashion ; but the slow person does not protract the thing because he wishes to spend more time about it, but because by his nature he requires more time, and if he made more haste would not do the thing so well. This time, therefore, depends on subjective causes, and belongs to the length, so called, of the action.

If we allow now to every action in War this, its length, then, every suspension of hostile action, appears an absurdity.

There is only one Cause which can suspend the Action, and this seems to be only Possible on One Side in any Case

If two parties have armed themselves for strife, then a feeling of animosity must have moved them to it ; as long now as they continue armed, that is, do not come to terms of peace, this feeling must exist, and it can only be brought to a standstill by either side by one single motive alone, which is, *that he waits for a more favourable moment for action.* Now, at first sight, it appears that this motive can never exist except on one side. If the one has an interest in acting, then the other must have an interest in waiting.

A complete equilibrium of forces can never produce a suspension of action, for during this suspension he who is the assailant must continue progressing ; for if we should imagine an equilibrium in this way, that he who has the strongest motive, can at the same time only command the lesser means, then we must say, the two parties must make peace. We see that the conception of an equilibrium cannot explain a suspension of arms, but that it ends in the question of the *expectation of a more favourable moment.*

Let us suppose, therefore, that one of two States has a positive object, as, for instance, the conquest of one of the enemy's provinces—which is to be utilized in the settlement of peace. After this conquest, his political object is accomplished, the necessity for action ceases, and for him a pause ensues. If the adversary is also contented with this solution, he will make peace ; if not, he must act. Now, if we suppose that in four weeks he will be in a better condition to act, then he has sufficient grounds for putting off the time of action.

But from that moment the logical course for the enemy appears to be to act that he may not give the conquered party *the desired* time. Of course, in this mode of reasoning a complete insight into the state of circumstances on both sides is supposed.

Thus a Continuance of Action will ensue which will Advance Towards a Climax

If this unbroken continuity of hostile operations really existed, the effect would be that everything would again be driven towards the extreme ; for, irrespective of the effect of such incessant activity in inflaming the feelings, and infusing into the whole a greater degree of passion, a greater elementary force, there would also follow from this continuance of action a stricter continuity, a closer connection between cause and effect, and thus every single action would become of more importance, and consequently more replete with danger.

But we know that the course of action in War has seldom or never this unbroken continuity, and that there have been many Wars in which action occupied by far the smallest portion of time employed, the whole of the rest being consumed in inaction. It is impossible that this should be always an anomaly ; suspension of action in War must therefore be possible, that is no contradiction in itself. We now proceed to show how this is.

Here, Therefore, the Principle of Polarity is Brought into Requisition

As we have supposed the interests of one Commander to be always antagonistic to those of the other, we have assumed a true *polarity*. We reserve a fuller explanation of this for another chapter, merely making the following observation on it at present.

The principle of polarity is only valid when it can be conceived in one and the same thing, where the positive and its opposite the negative completely destroy each other. In a battle both sides strive to conquer ; that is true polarity, for the victory of the one side destroys that of the other. But when we speak of two different things which have a common relation external to themselves, then it is not the things but their relations which have the polarity.

*Attack and Defence are Things Differing in Kind and of Unequal
Force. Polarity is, therefore, not Applicable to them*

If there was only one form of War, to wit, the attack of the
enemy, therefore no defence ; or, in other words, if the attack
was distinguished from the defence merely by the positive
motive, which the one has and the other has not, but the methods
of each were precisely one and the same : then in this sort of
fight every advantage gained on the one side would be a corresponding disadvantage on the other, and true polarity would
exist.

But action in War is divided into two forms, attack and
defence, which, as we shall hereafter explain more particularly,
are very different and of unequal strength. Polarity therefore
lies in that to which both bear a relation, in the decision, but
not in the attack or defence itself.

If the one Commander wishes the solution put off, the other
must wish to hasten it, but only by the same form of action.
If it is A's interest not to attack his enemy at present, but four
weeks hence, then it is B's interest to be attacked, not four
weeks hence, but at the present moment. This is the direct
antagonism of interests, but it by no means follows that it would
be for B's interest to attack A at once. That is plainly something
totally different.

*The Effect of Polarity is often Destroyed by the Superiority of the
Defence over the Attack, and thus the Suspension of Action in
War is Explained*

If the form of defence is stronger than that of offence, as we
shall hereafter show, the question arises, Is the advantage of a
deferred decision as great on the one side as the advantage of
the defensive form on the other ? If it is not, then it cannot
by its counterweight over-balance the latter, and thus influence
the progress of the action of the War. We see, therefore, that
the impulsive force existing in the polarity of interests may
be lost in the difference between the strength of the offensive
and the defensive, and thereby become ineffectual.

If, therefore, that side for which the present is favourable, is too weak to be able to dispense with the advantage of the defensive, he must put up with the unfavourable prospects which the future holds out ; for it may still be better to fight a defensive battle in the unpromising future than to assume the offensive or make peace at present. Now, being convinced that the superiority of the defensive (rightly understood) is very great, and much greater than may appear at first sight, we conceive that the greater number of those periods of inaction which occur in war are thus explained without involving any contradiction. The weaker the motives to action are, the more will those motives be absorbed and neutralised by this difference between attack and defence, the more frequently, therefore, will action in warfare be stopped, as indeed experience teaches.

A Second Ground consists in the Imperfect Knowledge of Circumstances

But there is still another cause which may stop action in War, viz., an incomplete view of the situation. Each Commander can only fully know his own position ; that of his opponent can only be known to him by reports, which are uncertain ; he may, therefore, form a wrong judgment with respect to it upon data of this description, and, in consequence of that error, he may suppose that the power of taking the initiative rests with his adversary when it lies really with himself. This want of perfect insight might certainly just as often occasion an untimely action as untimely inaction, and hence it would in itself no more contribute to delay than to accelerate action in War. Still, it must always be regarded as one of the natural causes which may bring action in War to a standstill without involving a contradiction. But if we reflect how much more we are inclined and induced to estimate the power of our opponents too high than too low, because it lies in human nature to do so, we shall admit that our imperfect insight into facts in general must contribute very much to delay action in War, and to modify the application of the principles pending our conduct.

The possibility of a standstill brings into the action of War a new modification, inasmuch as it dilutes that action with the element of time, checks the influence or sense of danger in its course, and increases the means of reinstating a lost balance of force. The greater the tension of feelings from which the War springs, the greater therefore the energy with which it is carried on, so much the shorter will be the periods of inaction ; on the other hand, the weaker the principle of warlike activity, the longer will be these periods : for powerful motives increase the force of the will, and this, as we know, is always a factor in the product of force.

Frequent Periods of Inaction in War remove it further from the Absolute, and make it still more a Calculation of Probabilities

But the slower the action proceeds in War, the more frequent and longer the periods of inaction, so much the more easily can an error be repaired ; therefore, so much the bolder a General will be in his calculations, so much the more readily will he build everything upon probabilities and conjecture. Thus, according as the course of the War is more or less slow, more or less time will be allowed for that which the nature of a concrete case particularly requires, calculation of probability based on given circumstances.

Therefore, the Element of Chance only is wanting to make of War a Game, and in that Element it is least of all Deficient

We see from the foregoing how much the objective nature of War makes it a calculation of probabilities ; now there is only one single element still wanting to make it a game, and that element it certainly is not without : it is chance. There is no human affair which stands so constantly and so generally in close connection with chance as War. But together with chance, the accidental, and along with it good luck, occupy a great place in War.

War is a Game both Objectively and Subjectively

If we now take a look at the *subjective nature* of War, that is to say, at those conditions under which it is carried on, it will appear to us still more like a game. Primarily the element in which the operations of War are carried on is danger ; but which of all the moral qualities is the first in danger ? *Courage.*

Now certainly courage is quite compatible with prudent calculation, but still they are things of quite a different kind, essentially different qualities of the mind ; on the other hand, daring reliance on good fortune, boldness, rashness, are only expressions of courage, and all these propensities of the mind look for the fortuitous (or accidental), because it is their element.

We see, therefore, how, from the commencement, the absolute, the mathematical as it is called, nowhere finds any sure basis in the calculations in the Art of War ; and that from the outset there is a play of possibilities, probabilities, good and bad luck, which spreads about with all the coarse and fine threads of its web, and makes War of all branches of human activity the most like a gambling game.

How this Accords best with the Human Mind in General

Although our intellect always feels itself urged towards clearness and certainty, still our mind often feels itself attracted by uncertainty. Instead of threading its way with the understanding along the narrow path of philosophical investigations and logical conclusions, in order, almost unconscious of itself, to arrive in spaces where it feels itself a stranger, and where it seems to part from all well-known objects, it prefers to remain with the imagination in the realms of chance and luck. Instead of living yonder on poor necessity, it revels here in the wealth of possibilities ; animated thereby, courage then takes wings to itself, and daring and danger make the element into which it launches itself as a fearless swimmer plunges into the stream.

Shall theory leave it here, and move on, self-satisfied with absolute conclusions and rules ? Then it is of no practical use. Theory must also take into account the human element ; it must accord a place to courage, to boldness, even to rashness. The Art of War has to deal with living and with moral forces, the consequence of which is that it can never attain the absolute and positive. There is therefore everywhere a margin for the accidental, and just as much in the greatest things as in the smallest. As there is room for this accidental on the one hand, so on the other there must be courage and self-reliance in proportion to the room available. If these qualities are forthcoming in a high degree, the margin left may likewise be great. Courage and self-reliance are, therefore, principles quite essential to War ; consequently, theory must only set up such rules as allow ample scope for all degrees and varieties of these necessary and noblest of military virtues. In daring there may still be wisdom, and prudence as well, only they are estimated by a different standard of value.

War is Always a Serious Means for a Serious Object. Its more Particular Definition

Such is War ; such the Commander who conducts it ; such the theory which rules it. But War is no pastime ; no mere passion for venturing and winning ; no work of a free enthusiasm : it is a serious means for a serious object. All that appearance which it wears from the varying hues of fortune, all that it assimilates into itself of the oscillations of passion, of courage, of imagination, of enthusiasm, are only particular properties of this means.

The War of a community—of whole Nations, and particularly of civilized Nations—always starts from a political condition, and is called forth by a political motive. It is, therefore, a political act. Now if it was a perfect, unrestrained, and absolute expression of force, as we had to deduce it from its mere conception, then the moment it is called forth by policy it would step into the place of policy, and as something quite independent of it would set it aside, and only follow its own laws, just as a mine at the moment of explosion cannot be guided into any other direction than that which has been given to it by preparatory arrangements. This is how the thing has really been viewed hitherto, whenever a want of harmony between policy and the conduct of a War has led to theoretical distinctions of the kind. But it is not so, and the idea is radically false. War in the real world, as we have already seen, is not an extreme thing which expends itself at one single discharge ; it is the operation of powers which do not develop themselves completely in the same manner and in the same measure, but which at one time expand sufficiently to overcome the resistance opposed by inertia or friction, while at another they are too weak to produce an effect ; it is therefore, in a certain measure, a pulsation of violent force more or less vehement, consequently making its discharges and exhausting its powers more or less quickly—in other words, conducting more or less quickly to the aim, but always lasting long enough to admit of influence being exerted on it in its course, so as to give it this or that direction. Now, if we reflect that War has its root in a political object, then naturally this original motive which called it into existence should also continue the first and highest consideration in its conduct. Still, the political object is no despotic lawgiver on that account ; it must accommodate itself to the nature of the means, and though changes in these means may involve modification in the political objective, the latter always retains a prior right to consideration. Policy, therefore, is interwoven with the whole action of War, and must exercise a continuous influence upon it, as far as the nature of the forces liberated by it will permit.

War is a Mere Continuation of Policy by Other Means

We see, therefore, that War is not merely a political act, but also a real political instrument, a continuation of political commerce, a carrying out of the same by other means. All beyond this which is strictly peculiar to War relates merely to the peculiar nature of the means which it uses. That the tendencies and views of policy shall not be incompatible with these means, the Art of War in general and the Commander in each particular case may demand, and this claim is truly not a trifling one. But however powerfully this may react on political views in particular cases, still it must always be regarded as only a modification of them ; for the political view is the object, War is the means, and the means must always include the object in our conception.

Diversity in the Nature of Wars

The greater and the more powerful the motives of a War, the more it affects the whole existence of a people. The more violent the excitement which precedes the War, by so much the nearer will the War approach to its abstract form, so much the more will it be directed to the destruction of the enemy, so much the nearer will the military and political ends coincide,

so much the more purely military and less political the War
appears to be ; but the weaker the motives and the tensions,
so much the less will the natural direction of the military
element—that is, force—be coincident with the direction
which the political element indicates ; so much the more must,
therefore, the War become diverted from its natural direction,
the political object diverge from the aim of an ideal War, and
the War appear to become political.

But, that the reader may not form any false conception, we
must here observe that by this natural tendency of War we only
mean the philosophical, the strictly logical, and by no means
the tendency of forces actually engaged in conflict, by which
would be supposed to be included all the emotions and passions
of the combatants. No doubt in some cases these also might
be excited to such a degree as to be with difficulty restrained
and confined to the political road ; but in most cases such a
contradiction will not arise, because by the existence of such
strenuous exertions a great plan in harmony therewith would
be implied. If the plan is directed only upon a small object,
then the impulses of feeling amongst the masses will be also so
weak that these masses will require to be stimulated rather than
repressed.

They may all be Regarded as Political Acts

Returning now to the main subject, although it is true that
in one kind of War the political element seems almost to disappear, whilst in another kind it occupies a very prominent
place, we may still affirm that the one is as political as the other.
It is only if we understand by policy not a true appreciation of
affairs in general, but the conventional conception of a cautious,
subtle, also dishonest craftiness, averse from violence, that the
latter kind of War may belong more to policy than the first.

Influence of this View on the Right Understanding of Military History, and on the Foundations of Theory

We see, therefore, in the first place, that under all circumstances War is to be regarded not as an independent thing, but
as a political instrument ; and it is only by taking this point

of view that we can avoid finding ourselves in opposition to all military history. This is the only means of unlocking the great book and making it intelligible. Secondly, this view shows us how Wars must differ in character according to the nature of the motives and circumstances from which they proceed.

Now, the first, the grandest, and most decisive act of judgment which the Statesman and General exercises is rightly to understand in this respect the War in which he engages, not to take it for something, or to wish to make of it something, which by the nature of its relations it is impossible for it to be. This is, therefore, the first, the most comprehensive, of all strategical questions.

Result for Theory

War is, therefore, not only chameleon-like in character, because it changes its colour in some degree in each particular case, but it is also, as a whole, in relation to the predominant tendencies which are in it, a strange trinity, composed of the original violence of its elements, hatred and animosity, which may be looked upon as blind instinct ; of the play of probabilities and chance, which make it a free activity of the soul ; and of the subordinate nature of a political instrument, by which it belongs purely to the reason.

The first of these three phases concerns more the people ; the second, more the General and his Army ; the third, more the Government. The passions which break forth in War must already have a latent existence in the peoples. The range which the display of courage and talents shall get in the realm of probabilities and of chance depends on the particular characteristics of the General and his Army, but the political objects belong to the Government alone.

These three tendencies, which appear like so many different law-givers, are deeply rooted in the nature of the subject, and at the same time variable in degree. A theory which would leave any one of them out of account, or set up any arbitrary relation between them, would immediately become involved in such a contradiction with the reality, that it might be regarded as destroyed at once by that alone.

The problem is, therefore, that theory shall keep itself poised in a manner between these three tendencies, as between three points of attraction.

The way in which alone this difficult probelm can be solved we shall examine in the book on the *Theory of War*. At any rate, the conception of War, as here defined, will be the first ray of light which shows us the true foundation of theory, and which first separates the great masses and allows us to distinguish them from one another.

END AND MEANS IN WAR

Having in the foregoing section ascertained the complicated and variable nature of War, we shall now occupy ourselves with examining the influence which this nature has upon the end and means in War.

If we ask, first of all, for the object upon which the whole effort of War is to be directed, in order that it may suffice for the attainment of the political object, we shall find that it is just as variable as are the political object and the particular circumstances of the War.

If, in the next place, we keep once more to the pure conception of War, then we must say that the political object properly lies out of its province, for if War is an act of violence to compel the enemy to fulfil our will, then in every case all depends on our overthrowing the enemy, that is, disarming him, and on that alone.

We shall hereafter examine more closely into the meaning of disarming a nation, but here we must at once draw a distinction between three things, which, as three general objects, comprise everything else within them. They are the *military power, the country,* and *the will of the enemy*.

The *military power* must be destroyed, that is, reduced to such a state as not to be able to prosecute the War. This is the sense in which we wish to be understood hereafter, whenever we use the expression " destruction of the enemy's military power."

The *country* must be conquered, for out of the country a new military force may be formed.

But even when both these things are done, still the War,

that is, the hostile feeling and action of hostile agencies, cannot be considered as at an end as long as the *will* of the enemy is not subdued also ; that is, its Government and its Allies must be forced into signing a peace, or the people into submission ; for whilst we are in full occupation of the country, the War may break out afresh, either in the interior or through assistance given by Allies. No doubt, this may also take place after a peace, but that shows nothing more than that every War does not carry in itself the elements for a complete decision and final settlement.

But even if this is the case, still with the conclusion of peace a number of sparks are always extinguished which would have smouldered on quietly, and the excitement of the passions abates, because all those whose minds are disposed to peace, of which in all nations and under all circumstances there is always a great number, turn themselves away completely from the road to resistance. Whatever may take place subsequently, we must always look upon the object as attained, and the business of War as ended, by a peace.

As protection of the country is the primary object for which the military force exists, therefore the natural order is, that first of all this force should be destroyed, then the country subdued.

But this object of War in the abstract, this final means of attaining the political object in which all others are combined, the *disarming the enemy*, is rarely attained in practice and is not a condition necessary to peace. There are innumerable instances of treaties in which peace has been settled before either party could be looked upon as disarmed ; indeed, even before the balance of power had undergone any sensible alteration.

There are two considerations which as motives may practically take the place of inability to continue the contest. The first is the improbability, the second is the excessive price, of success.

War does not always require to be fought out until one party is overthrown ; when the motives and passions are slight, a weak probability will suffice to move that side to which it is unfavourable to give way. Now, were the other side convinced of this beforehand, it is natural that he would strive for this probability only, instead of first wasting time and effort in the attempt to achieve the total destruction of the enemy's Army.

Still more general in its influence on the resolution to peace is the consideration of the expenditure of force already made, and further required. As War is no act of blind passion, but is dominated by the political object, therefore the value of that object determines the measure of the sacrifices by which it is to be purchased. This will be the case, not only as regards extent, but also as regards duration. As soon, therefore, as the required outlay becomes so great that the political object is no longer equal in value, the object must be given up, and peace will be the result.

We see, therefore, that in Wars where one side cannot completely disarm the other, the motives to peace on both sides will rise or fall on each side according to the probability of future success and the required outlay. If these motives were equally strong on both sides, they would meet in the centre of their political difference. Where they are strong on one side, they might be weak on the other. If their amount is only sufficient, peace will follow, but naturally to the advantage of that side which has the weakest motive for its conclusion.

Now comes the question how to influence the probability of success. In the first place, by the destruction of the enemy's military force and the conquest of his provinces ; but these two means are not exactly of the same import here. If we attack the enemy's Army, it is a very different thing whether we intend to follow up the first blow with a succession of others, until the whole force is destroyed, or whether we mean to content ourselves with a victory to shake the enemy's feeling of security, to convince him of our superiority, and to instil into him a feeling of apprehension about the future. If this is our object, we only go so far in the destruction of his forces as is sufficient. In like manner, the conquest of the enemy's provinces is quite a different measure if the object is not the destruction of the enemy's Army. In the latter case the destruction of the Army is the real effectual action, and the taking of the provinces only a consequence of it ; to take them before the Army had been defeated would always be looked upon only as a necessary evil. On the other hand, if our views are not directed upon the complete destruction of the enemy's force, and if we are sure that the enemy does not seek but fears to bring matters to a bloody decision, the taking possession of a weak or defenceless province is an advantage in itself, and if this advantage is of sufficient importance to make the enemy apprehensive about the general result, then it may also be regarded as a shorter road to peace.

But now we come upon a peculiar means of influencing the probability of the result without destroying the enemy's Army, namely, upon the expeditions which have a direct connection with political views. If there are any enterprises which are particularly likely to break up the enemy's alliances or make them inoperative, to gain new alliances for ourselves, to raise political powers in our own favour, etc., etc., then it is easy to conceive how much these may increase the probability of success, and become a shorter way towards our object than the routing of the enemy's forces.

The second question is how to act upon the enemy's expenditure in strength, that is, to raise the price of success.

The enemy's outlay in strength lies in the *wear and tear* of his forces, consequently in the *destruction* of them on our part, and in the *loss of provinces*, consequently the *conquest* of them by us.

Besides these two means, there are three other peculiar ways of directly increasing the waste of the enemy's force. The first is *invasion*, that is *the occupation of the enemy's territory, not with a view to keeping it*, but in order to levy contributions upon it, or to devastate it.

The immediate object here is neither the conquest of the enemy's territory nor the defeat of his armed force, but merely to *do him damage in a general way*, The second way is to select for the object of our enterprises those points at which we can do the enemy most harm. The third, by far the most important, from the great number of cases which it embraces, is the *wearing out* of the enemy. The idea of wearing out in a struggle amounts in practice to *a gradual exhaustion of the physical powers and of the will by the long continuance of exertion*.

Now, if we want to overcome the enemy by the duration of the contest, we must content ourselves with as small objects as possible ; the smallest object that we can propose to ourselves is simple passive resistance, that is a combat without any positive view. In this way, our means attain their greatest relative value, and therefore the result is best secured. How far now can this negative mode of proceeding be carried ?

Plainly not to absolute passivity, for mere endurance would not be fighting ; and the defensive is an activity by which so much of the enemy's power must be destroyed that he must give up his object. That alone is what we aim at in each single act, and therein consists the negative nature of our object.

No doubt this negative object is not so effective as the positive object in the same direction would be ; but it holds out greater certainty of success ; what is wanting in the efficacy of its single act must be gained through time, that is, through the duration of the contest, and therefore this negative intention, which constitutes the principle of the pure defensive, is also the natural means of wearing the enemy out.

Here lies the origin of that difference of *Offensive* and *Defensive*, the influence of which prevails throughout the whole province of War. From this negative intention are to be deduced all the advantages and all the stronger forms of combat which are on the side of the *Defensive*, and in which that philosophical-dynamic law which exists between the greatness and the certainty of success is realized.

If then the concentration of all the means into a state of pure resistance, affords a superiority in the contest, and if this advantage is sufficient to *balance* whatever superiority in numbers the adversary may have, then the mere *duration* of the contest will suffice gradually to bring the loss of force on the part of the adversary to a point at which the political object can no longer be an equivalent, a point at which, therefore, he must give up the contest. We see then that this class of means, the wearing out of the enemy, includes the great number of cases in which the weaker resists the stronger.

We see that there are many ways to one's object in War ; that the complete subjugation of the enemy is not essential in every case ; that the destruction of the enemy's military force, the conquest of the enemy's provinces, the mere occupation of them, the mere invasion of them—enterprises which are aimed directly at political objects—lastly, a passive expectation of the enemy's blow, are all means which, each in itself, may be used to force the enemy's will according as the peculiar circumstances of the case lead us to expect more from the one or the other. We could still add to these a whole category of shorter methods of gaining the end, which might be called arguments *ad hominem*.

What branch of human affairs is there in which these sparks of individual spirit have not made their appearance, surmounting all formal considerations ? And least of all can they fail to appear in War, where the personal character of the combatants plays such an important part, both in the cabinet and in the field. We limit ourselves to pointing this out, as it would be pedantry to attempt to reduce such influences into classes. Including these, we may say that the number of possible ways of reaching the object rises to infinity.

To avoid underestimating these different short roads to one's purpose, we must bear in mind the diversity of political objects which may cause a War—measure at a glance the distance which there is between a death struggle for political existence and a War which a forced or tottering alliance makes a matter of disagreeable duty. Between the two innumerable gradations occur in practice. If we reject one of these gradations in theory, we might with equal right reject the whole, which would be tantamount to shutting the real world completely out of sight.

These are the circumstances in general connected with the aim which we have to pursue in War ; let us now turn to the means.

There is only single means, it is the *Fight*. However diversified this may be in form, however widely it may differ from a rough vent of hatred and animosity in a hand-to-hand encounter, whatever number of things may introduce themselves which are not actual fighting, still it is always implied in the conception of War that all the effects manifested have their roots in the combat.

That this must always be so in the greatest diversity and complication of the reality is proved in a very simple manner. All that takes place in War takes place through armed forces, but where the forces of War, *i.e.*, armed men, are applied, there the idea of fighting must of necessity be at the foundation.

All, therefore, that relates to forces of War—all that is connected with their creation, maintenance, and application—belongs to military activity.

If the idea of combat lies at the foundation of every application of armed power, then also the application of armed force in general is nothing more than the determining and arranging a certain number of combats.

Every activity in War, therefore, necessarily relates to the combat either directly or indirectly. The soldier is levied, clothed, armed, exercised, he sleeps, eats, drinks, and marches, all *merely to fight at the right time and place.*

If, therefore, all the threads of military activity terminate in the combat, we shall grasp them all when we settle the order of the combats. In the combat all the action is directed to the *destruction* of the enemy, or rather of *his fighting powers.*

The object may likewise be the mere destruction of the enemy's armed force ; but that is not by any means necessary, and it may be something quite different. Whenever, for instance, as we have shown, the defeat of the enemy is not the only means to attain the political object, whenever there are other objects which may be pursued as the aim in a War, then it follows of itself that such other objects may become the object of particular acts of Warfare, and therefore also the object of combats.

But even those combats which, as subordinate acts, are in the strict sense devoted to the destruction of the enemy's fighting force need not have that destruction itself as their first object.

If we think of the manifold parts of a great armed force, of the number of circumstances which come into activity when it is employed, then it is clear that the combat of such a force must also require a manifold organization. There may and must naturally arise for particular parts a number of objects which are not themselves the destruction of the enemy's armed force, and which, while they certainly contribute to increase that destruction, do so only in an indirect manner. If a battalion is ordered to drive the enemy from a rising ground, or a bridge, etc., then properly the occupation of any such locality is the real object, the destruction of the enemy's armed force which takes place only the means or secondary matter. If the enemy can be driven away merely by a demonstration, the object is attained all the same ; but this hill or bridge is, in point of fact, only required as a means of increasing the gross amount of loss inflicted on the enemy's armed force. If this is the case on the field of battle, much more must it be so on the whole theatre of war, where not only one Army is opposed to another, but one State, one Nation, one whole country to another. Here the number of possible relations, and consequently possible combinations, is much greater, the diversity of measures increased.

It is therefore for many reasons possible that the object of a combat is not the destruction of the enemy's force. But in all such cases, the combat is nothing else but a measure of strength—has in itself no value except only that of the present result, that is, of its decision.

But a measuring of strength may be effected in cases where the opposing sides are very unequal by a mere comparative estimate. In such cases no fighting will take place, and the weaker will immediately give way.

If the object of a combat can often be attained as well without the combat taking place at all, by merely making a resolve to fight, then that explains how a whole campaign may be carried on with great activity without the actual combat playing any notable part in it.

That this may be so military history proves by a hundred examples. How many of those cases can be justified, that is, without involving a contradiction, and whether some of the celebrities who rose out of them would stand criticism, we shall leave undecided.

We have only one means in War—the battle ; from this means proceeds a thread which assists the study of the subject as it runs through the whole web of military activity and holds it together.

But we have considered the destruction of the enemy's force as one of the objects which may be pursued in War, and left undecided what relative importance should be given to it amongst other objects. We shall be able to get an insight into the value which must necessarily be accorded to it.

The combat is the single activity in War ; in the combat the destruction of the enemy opposed to us is the means to the end ; it is so even when the combat does not actually take place, because in that case there lies at the root of the decision the supposition at all events that this destruction is to be regarded as beyond doubt. It follows, therefore, that the destruction of the enemy's military force is the foundation-stone of all action in War.

The decision by arms is, for all operations in War, great and small, what cash payment is in bill transactions. However remote from each other these relations, however seldom the realization may take place, still it can never entirely fail to occur.

If the decision by arms lies at the foundation of all combinations, then it follows that the enemy can defeat each of them by gaining a victory on the field, not merely in the one on which our combination directly depends, but also in any other encounter, if it is only important enough ; for every important decision by arms—that is, destruction of the enemy's forces—reacts upon all preceding it, because, like a liquid element, they tend to bring themselves to a level.

Thus, the destruction of the enemy's armed force appears, therefore, always as the superior and more effectual means, to which all others must give way.

It is, however, only when there is a supposed equality in all other conditions that we can ascribe to the destruction of the enemy's armed force the greater efficacy. It would, therefore, be a great mistake to draw the conclusion that a blind dash must always gain the victory over skill and caution. An unskilful attack would lead to the destruction of our own and not of the enemy's force, and therefore is not what is here meant. The superior efficacy belongs not to the *means* but to the *end*.

If we speak of the destruction of the enemy's armed force, we must expressly point out that nothing obliges us to confine this idea to the mere physical force ; on the contrary, the moral is necessarily implied as well, because both in fact are interwoven with each other, even in the most minute details, and therefore cannot be separated. But it is just in connection with the inevitable effect which has been referred to, of a great act of destruction (a great victory) upon all other decisions by arms, that this moral element is most fluid, if we may use that expression, and therefore distributes itself the most easily through all the parts.

Against the far superior worth which the destruction of the enemy's armed force has over all other means stands the expense and risk of this means, and it is only to avoid these that any other means are taken.

The danger lies in this, that the greater efficacy which we seek recoils on ourselves, and therefore has worse consequences in case we fail of success.

Other methods are, therefore, less costly when they succeed, less dangerous when they fail ; but in this is necessarily lodged the condition that they are only opposed to similar ones, that is, that the enemy acts on the same principle ; for if the enemy should choose the way of a great decision by arms, *our means must on that account be changed against our will, in order to correspond with his.* Then all depends on the issue of the act of destruction ; but of course it is evident that, *ceteris paribus,* in this act we must be at a disadvantage in all respects because our views and our means had been directed in part upon other objects, which is not the case with the enemy. If, therefore, one of two belligerents is determined to seek the great decision by arms, then he has a high probability of success, as soon as he is certain his opponent will not take that way, but follows a different object ; and every one who sets before himself any such other aim only does so in a reasonable manner, provided he acts on the supposition that his adversary has as little intention as he has of resorting to the great decision by arms.

But what we have here said of another direction of views and forces relates only to other *positive objects,* which we may propose to ourselves in War, besides the destruction of the enemy's force, not by any means to the pure defensive, which may be adopted with a view thereby to exhaust the enemy's forces. In the pure defensive the positive object is wanting, and therefore, while on the defensive, our forces cannot at the same time be directed on other objects ; they can only be employed to defeat the intentions of the enemy.

We have now to consider the opposite of the destruction of the enemy's armed force, that is to say, the preservation of our own. These two efforts always go together, as they mutually act and react on each other ; we have only to ascertain what effect is produced when one or the other has the predominance. The endeavour to destroy the enemy's force has a positive object, and leads to positive results, of which the final aim is the conquest of the enemy. The preservation of our own forces has a negative object, leads therefore to the defeat of the enemy's intentions, that is to pure resistance, of which the final aim can be nothing more than to prolong the duration of the contest, so that the enemy shall exhaust himself in it.

The effort with a positive object calls into existence the act of destruction ; the effort with the negative object awaits it.

How far this state of expectation should and may be carried we shall enter into more particularly in the theory of attack and defence. Here we shall content ouselves with saying that the awaiting must be no absolute endurance, and that in the action bound up with it the destruction of the enemy's armed force may be the aim just as well as anything else. It would therefore be a great error in the fundamental idea to suppose that the consequence of the negative course is that we are precluded from choosing the destruction of the enemy's military force as our object, and must prefer a bloodless solution. The advantage which the negative effort gives may certainly lead to that, but only at the risk of its not being the most advisable method. This other bloodless way cannot, therefore, be looked upon at all as the natural means of satisfying our great anxiety to spare our forces ; on the contrary, when circumstances are not favourable, it would be the means of completely ruining them. Very many Generals have fallen into this error, and been ruined by it.

We have seen, therefore, in the foregoing reflections, that there are many ways to the aim, that is, to the attainment of the political object ; but that the only means is the combat, and that consequently everything is subject to a supreme law : which is the *decision by arms* ; the destruction of the enemy's armed force, amongst all the objects which can be pursued in War, appears always as the one which overrules all others.

What may be achieved by combinations of another kind in War we shall only learn in the sequel, and naturally only by degrees. If when political objects are unimportant, motives weak, the tension of forces small, a cautious commander tries in all kinds of ways, without great crises and bloody solutions, to twist himself skilfully into a peace through the characteristic weaknesses of his enemy in the field and in the Cabinet, we have no right to find fault with him, if the premises on which he acts are well founded and justified by success ; still we must require him to remember that he only travels on forbidden tracks, where the God of War may surprise him ; that he ought always to keep his eye on the enemy, in order that he may not have to defend himself with a dress rapier if the enemy takes up a sharp sword.

A CATALOG OF SELECTED DOVER
BOOKS IN ALL FIELDS OF INTEREST

CONCERNING THE SPIRITUAL IN ART, Wassily Kandinsky. Pioneering work by father of abstract art. Thoughts on color theory, nature of art. Analysis of earlier masters. 12 illustrations. 80pp. of text. 5⅜ x 8½.   23411-8

ANIMALS: 1,419 Copyright-Free Illustrations of Mammals, Birds, Fish, Insects, etc., Jim Harter (ed.). Clear wood engravings present, in extremely lifelike poses, over 1,000 species of animals. One of the most extensive pictorial sourcebooks of its kind. Captions. Index. 284pp. 9 x 12.   23766-4

CELTIC ART: The Methods of Construction, George Bain. Simple geometric techniques for making Celtic interlacements, spirals, Kells-type initials, animals, humans, etc. Over 500 illustrations. 160pp. 9 x 12. (Available in U.S. only.)   22923-8

AN ATLAS OF ANATOMY FOR ARTISTS, Fritz Schider. Most thorough reference work on art anatomy in the world. Hundreds of illustrations, including selections from works by Vesalius, Leonardo, Goya, Ingres, Michelangelo, others. 593 illustrations. 192pp. 7⅛ x 10¼.   20241-0

CELTIC HAND STROKE-BY-STROKE (Irish Half-Uncial from "The Book of Kells"): An Arthur Baker Calligraphy Manual, Arthur Baker. Complete guide to creating each letter of the alphabet in distinctive Celtic manner. Covers hand position, strokes, pens, inks, paper, more. Illustrated. 48pp. 8¼ x 11.   24336-2

EASY ORIGAMI, John Montroll. Charming collection of 32 projects (hat, cup, pelican, piano, swan, many more) specially designed for the novice origami hobbyist. Clearly illustrated easy-to-follow instructions insure that even beginning papercrafters will achieve successful results. 48pp. 8¼ x 11.   27298-2

THE COMPLETE BOOK OF BIRDHOUSE CONSTRUCTION FOR WOODWORKERS, Scott D. Campbell. Detailed instructions, illustrations, tables. Also data on bird habitat and instinct patterns. Bibliography. 3 tables. 63 illustrations in 15 figures. 48pp. 5¼ x 8½.   24407-5

BLOOMINGDALE'S ILLUSTRATED 1886 CATALOG: Fashions, Dry Goods and Housewares, Bloomingdale Brothers. Famed merchants' extremely rare catalog depicting about 1,700 products: clothing, housewares, firearms, dry goods, jewelry, more. Invaluable for dating, identifying vintage items. Also, copyright-free graphics for artists, designers. Co-published with Henry Ford Museum & Greenfield Village. 160pp. 8¼ x 11.   25780-0

HISTORIC COSTUME IN PICTURES, Braun & Schneider. Over 1,450 costumed figures in clearly detailed engravings–from dawn of civilization to end of 19th century. Captions. Many folk costumes. 256pp. 8⅜ x 11¾.   23150-X

STICKLEY CRAFTSMAN FURNITURE CATALOGS, Gustav Stickley and L. & J. G. Stickley. Beautiful, functional furniture in two authentic catalogs from 1910. 594 illustrations, including 277 photos, show settles, rockers, armchairs, reclining chairs, bookcases, desks, tables. 183pp. 6½ x 9¼. 23838-5

AMERICAN LOCOMOTIVES IN HISTORIC PHOTOGRAPHS: 1858 to 1949, Ron Ziel (ed.). A rare collection of 126 meticulously detailed official photographs, called "builder portraits," of American locomotives that majestically chronicle the rise of steam locomotive power in America. Introduction. Detailed captions. xi+ 129pp. 9 x 12. 27393-8

AMERICA'S LIGHTHOUSES: An Illustrated History, Francis Ross Holland, Jr. Delightfully written, profusely illustrated fact-filled survey of over 200 American lighthouses since 1716. History, anecdotes, technological advances, more. 240pp. 8 x 10¾. 25576-X

TOWARDS A NEW ARCHITECTURE, Le Corbusier. Pioneering manifesto by founder of "International School." Technical and aesthetic theories, views of industry, economics, relation of form to function, "mass-production split" and much more. Profusely illustrated. 320pp. 6⅛ x 9¼. (Available in U.S. only.) 25023-7

HOW THE OTHER HALF LIVES, Jacob Riis. Famous journalistic record, exposing poverty and degradation of New York slums around 1900, by major social reformer. 100 striking and influential photographs. 233pp. 10 x 7⅞. 22012-5

FRUIT KEY AND TWIG KEY TO TREES AND SHRUBS, William M. Harlow. One of the handiest and most widely used identification aids. Fruit key covers 120 deciduous and evergreen species; twig key 160 deciduous species. Easily used. Over 300 photographs. 126pp. 5⅜ x 8½. 20511-8

COMMON BIRD SONGS, Dr. Donald J. Borror. Songs of 60 most common U.S. birds: robins, sparrows, cardinals, bluejays, finches, more–arranged in order of increasing complexity. Up to 9 variations of songs of each species.
Cassette and manual 99911-4

ORCHIDS AS HOUSE PLANTS, Rebecca Tyson Northen. Grow cattleyas and many other kinds of orchids–in a window, in a case, or under artificial light. 63 illustrations. 148pp. 5⅜ x 8½. 23261-1

MONSTER MAZES, Dave Phillips. Masterful mazes at four levels of difficulty. Avoid deadly perils and evil creatures to find magical treasures. Solutions for all 32 exciting illustrated puzzles. 48pp. 8¼ x 11. 26005-4

MOZART'S DON GIOVANNI (DOVER OPERA LIBRETTO SERIES), Wolfgang Amadeus Mozart. Introduced and translated by Ellen H. Bleiler. Standard Italian libretto, with complete English translation. Convenient and thoroughly portable–an ideal companion for reading along with a recording or the performance itself. Introduction. List of characters. Plot summary. 121pp. 5¼ x 8½. 24944-1

TECHNICAL MANUAL AND DICTIONARY OF CLASSICAL BALLET, Gail Grant. Defines, explains, comments on steps, movements, poses and concepts. 15-page pictorial section. Basic book for student, viewer. 127pp. 5⅜ x 8½. 21843-0

THE CLARINET AND CLARINET PLAYING, David Pino. Lively, comprehensive work features suggestions about technique, musicianship, and musical interpretation, as well as guidelines for teaching, making your own reeds, and preparing for public performance. Includes an intriguing look at clarinet history. "A godsend," *The Clarinet,* Journal of the International Clarinet Society. Appendixes. 7 illus. 320pp. 5⅜ x 8½. 40270-3

HOLLYWOOD GLAMOR PORTRAITS, John Kobal (ed.). 145 photos from 1926-49. Harlow, Gable, Bogart, Bacall; 94 stars in all. Full background on photographers, technical aspects. 160pp. 8⅜ x 11¼. 23352-9

THE ANNOTATED CASEY AT THE BAT: A Collection of Ballads about the Mighty Casey/Third, Revised Edition, Martin Gardner (ed.). Amusing sequels and parodies of one of America's best-loved poems: Casey's Revenge, Why Casey Whiffed, Casey's Sister at the Bat, others. 256pp. 5⅜ x 8½. 28598-7

THE RAVEN AND OTHER FAVORITE POEMS, Edgar Allan Poe. Over 40 of the author's most memorable poems: "The Bells," "Ulalume," "Israfel," "To Helen," "The Conqueror Worm," "Eldorado," "Annabel Lee," many more. Alphabetic lists of titles and first lines. 64pp. 5 3/16 x 8¼. 26685-0

PERSONAL MEMOIRS OF U. S. GRANT, Ulysses Simpson Grant. Intelligent, deeply moving firsthand account of Civil War campaigns, considered by many the finest military memoirs ever written. Includes letters, historic photographs, maps and more. 528pp. 6⅛ x 9¼. 28587-1

ANCIENT EGYPTIAN MATERIALS AND INDUSTRIES, A. Lucas and J. Harris. Fascinating, comprehensive, thoroughly documented text describes this ancient civilization's vast resources and the processes that incorporated them in daily life, including the use of animal products, building materials, cosmetics, perfumes and incense, fibers, glazed ware, glass and its manufacture, materials used in the mummification process, and much more. 544pp. 6⅛ x 9¼. (Available in U.S. only.) 40446-3

RUSSIAN STORIES/RUSSKIE RASSKAZY: A Dual-Language Book, edited by Gleb Struve. Twelve tales by such masters as Chekhov, Tolstoy, Dostoevsky, Pushkin, others. Excellent word-for-word English translations on facing pages, plus teaching and study aids, Russian/English vocabulary, biographical/critical introductions, more. 416pp. 5⅜ x 8½. 26244-8

PHILADELPHIA THEN AND NOW: 60 Sites Photographed in the Past and Present, Kenneth Finkel and Susan Oyama. Rare photographs of City Hall, Logan Square, Independence Hall, Betsy Ross House, other landmarks juxtaposed with contemporary views. Captures changing face of historic city. Introduction. Captions. 128pp. 8¼ x 11. 25790-8

AIA ARCHITECTURAL GUIDE TO NASSAU AND SUFFOLK COUNTIES, LONG ISLAND, The American Institute of Architects, Long Island Chapter, and the Society for the Preservation of Long Island Antiquities. Comprehensive, well-researched and generously illustrated volume brings to life over three centuries of Long Island's great architectural heritage. More than 240 photographs with authoritative, extensively detailed captions. 176pp. 8¼ x 11. 26946-9

NORTH AMERICAN INDIAN LIFE: Customs and Traditions of 23 Tribes, Elsie Clews Parsons (ed.). 27 fictionalized essays by noted anthropologists examine religion, customs, government, additional facets of life among the Winnebago, Crow, Zuni, Eskimo, other tribes. 480pp. 6⅛ x 9¼. 27377-6

FRANK LLOYD WRIGHT'S DANA HOUSE, Donald Hoffmann. Pictorial essay of residential masterpiece with over 160 interior and exterior photos, plans, elevations, sketches and studies. 128pp. 9¼ x 10¾. 29120-0

THE MALE AND FEMALE FIGURE IN MOTION: 60 Classic Photographic Sequences, Eadweard Muybridge. 60 true-action photographs of men and women walking, running, climbing, bending, turning, etc., reproduced from rare 19th-century masterpiece. vi + 121pp. 9 x 12. 24745-7

1001 QUESTIONS ANSWERED ABOUT THE SEASHORE, N. J. Berrill and Jacquelyn Berrill. Queries answered about dolphins, sea snails, sponges, starfish, fishes, shore birds, many others. Covers appearance, breeding, growth, feeding, much more. 305pp. 5¼ x 8¼. 23366-9

ATTRACTING BIRDS TO YOUR YARD, William J. Weber. Easy-to-follow guide offers advice on how to attract the greatest diversity of birds: birdhouses, feeders, water and waterers, much more. 96pp. 5³⁄₁₆ x 8¼. 28927-3

MEDICINAL AND OTHER USES OF NORTH AMERICAN PLANTS: A Historical Survey with Special Reference to the Eastern Indian Tribes, Charlotte Erichsen-Brown. Chronological historical citations document 500 years of usage of plants, trees, shrubs native to eastern Canada, northeastern U.S. Also complete identifying information. 343 illustrations. 544pp. 6½ x 9¼. 25951-X

STORYBOOK MAZES, Dave Phillips. 23 stories and mazes on two-page spreads: Wizard of Oz, Treasure Island, Robin Hood, etc. Solutions. 64pp. 8¼ x 11. 23628-5

AMERICAN NEGRO SONGS: 230 Folk Songs and Spirituals, Religious and Secular, John W. Work. This authoritative study traces the African influences of songs sung and played by black Americans at work, in church, and as entertainment. The author discusses the lyric significance of such songs as "Swing Low, Sweet Chariot," "John Henry," and others and offers the words and music for 230 songs. Bibliography. Index of Song Titles. 272pp. 6½ x 9¼. 40271-1

MOVIE-STAR PORTRAITS OF THE FORTIES, John Kobal (ed.). 163 glamor, studio photos of 106 stars of the 1940s: Rita Hayworth, Ava Gardner, Marlon Brando, Clark Gable, many more. 176pp. 8⅜ x 11¼. 23546-7

BENCHLEY LOST AND FOUND, Robert Benchley. Finest humor from early 30s, about pet peeves, child psychologists, post office and others. Mostly unavailable elsewhere. 73 illustrations by Peter Arno and others. 183pp. 5⅜ x 8½. 22410-4

YEKL and THE IMPORTED BRIDEGROOM AND OTHER STORIES OF YIDDISH NEW YORK, Abraham Cahan. Film Hester Street based on *Yekl* (1896). Novel, other stories among first about Jewish immigrants on N.Y.'s East Side. 240pp. 5⅜ x 8½. 22427-9

SELECTED POEMS, Walt Whitman. Generous sampling from *Leaves of Grass*. Twenty-four poems include "I Hear America Singing," "Song of the Open Road," "I Sing the Body Electric," "When Lilacs Last in the Dooryard Bloom'd," "O Captain! My Captain!"—all reprinted from an authoritative edition. Lists of titles and first lines. 128pp. 5³⁄₁₆ x 8¼. 26878-0

THE BEST TALES OF HOFFMANN, E. T. A. Hoffmann. 10 of Hoffmann's most important stories: "Nutcracker and the King of Mice," "The Golden Flowerpot," etc. 458pp. 5⅜ x 8½. 21793-0

FROM FETISH TO GOD IN ANCIENT EGYPT, E. A. Wallis Budge. Rich detailed survey of Egyptian conception of "God" and gods, magic, cult of animals, Osiris, more. Also, superb English translations of hymns and legends. 240 illustrations. 545pp. 5⅜ x 8½. 25803-3

FRENCH STORIES/CONTES FRANÇAIS: A Dual-Language Book, Wallace Fowlie. Ten stories by French masters, Voltaire to Camus: "Micromegas" by Voltaire; "The Atheist's Mass" by Balzac; "Minuet" by de Maupassant; "The Guest" by Camus, six more. Excellent English translations on facing pages. Also French-English vocabulary list, exercises, more. 352pp. 5⅜ x 8½. 26443-2

CHICAGO AT THE TURN OF THE CENTURY IN PHOTOGRAPHS: 122 Historic Views from the Collections of the Chicago Historical Society, Larry A. Viskochil. Rare large-format prints offer detailed views of City Hall, State Street, the Loop, Hull House, Union Station, many other landmarks, circa 1904-1913. Introduction. Captions. Maps. 144pp. 9⅜ x 12¼. 24656-6

OLD BROOKLYN IN EARLY PHOTOGRAPHS, 1865-1929, William Lee Younger. Luna Park, Gravesend race track, construction of Grand Army Plaza, moving of Hotel Brighton, etc. 157 previously unpublished photographs. 165pp. 8⅞ x 11¾. 23587-4

THE MYTHS OF THE NORTH AMERICAN INDIANS, Lewis Spence. Rich anthology of the myths and legends of the Algonquins, Iroquois, Pawnees and Sioux, prefaced by an extensive historical and ethnological commentary. 36 illustrations. 480pp. 5⅜ x 8½. 25967-6

AN ENCYCLOPEDIA OF BATTLES: Accounts of Over 1,560 Battles from 1479 B.C. to the Present, David Eggenberger. Essential details of every major battle in recorded history from the first battle of Megiddo in 1479 B.C. to Grenada in 1984. List of Battle Maps. New Appendix covering the years 1967-1984. Index. 99 illustrations. 544pp. 6½ x 9¼. 24913-1

SAILING ALONE AROUND THE WORLD, Captain Joshua Slocum. First man to sail around the world, alone, in small boat. One of great feats of seamanship told in delightful manner. 67 illustrations. 294pp. 5⅜ x 8½. 20326-3

ANARCHISM AND OTHER ESSAYS, Emma Goldman. Powerful, penetrating, prophetic essays on direct action, role of minorities, prison reform, puritan hypocrisy, violence, etc. 271pp. 5⅜ x 8½. 22484-8

MYTHS OF THE HINDUS AND BUDDHISTS, Ananda K. Coomaraswamy and Sister Nivedita. Great stories of the epics; deeds of Krishna, Shiva, taken from puranas, Vedas, folk tales; etc. 32 illustrations. 400pp. 5⅜ x 8½. 21759-0

THE TRAUMA OF BIRTH, Otto Rank. Rank's controversial thesis that anxiety neurosis is caused by profound psychological trauma which occurs at birth. 256pp. 5⅜ x 8½. 27974-X

A THEOLOGICO-POLITICAL TREATISE, Benedict Spinoza. Also contains unfinished Political Treatise. Great classic on religious liberty, theory of government on common consent. R. Elwes translation. Total of 421pp. 5⅜ x 8½. 20249-6

MY BONDAGE AND MY FREEDOM, Frederick Douglass. Born a slave, Douglass became outspoken force in antislavery movement. The best of Douglass' autobiographies. Graphic description of slave life. 464pp. 5⅜ x 8½. 22457-0

FOLLOWING THE EQUATOR: A Journey Around the World, Mark Twain. Fascinating humorous account of 1897 voyage to Hawaii, Australia, India, New Zealand, etc. Ironic, bemused reports on peoples, customs, climate, flora and fauna, politics, much more. 197 illustrations. 720pp. 5⅜ x 8½. 26113-1

THE PEOPLE CALLED SHAKERS, Edward D. Andrews. Definitive study of Shakers: origins, beliefs, practices, dances, social organization, furniture and crafts, etc. 33 illustrations. 351pp. 5⅜ x 8½. 21081-2

THE MYTHS OF GREECE AND ROME, H. A. Guerber. A classic of mythology, generously illustrated, long prized for its simple, graphic, accurate retelling of the principal myths of Greece and Rome, and for its commentary on their origins and significance. With 64 illustrations by Michelangelo, Raphael, Titian, Rubens, Canova, Bernini and others. 480pp. 5⅜ x 8½. 27584-1

PSYCHOLOGY OF MUSIC, Carl E. Seashore. Classic work discusses music as a medium from psychological viewpoint. Clear treatment of physical acoustics, auditory apparatus, sound perception, development of musical skills, nature of musical feeling, host of other topics. 88 figures. 408pp. 5⅜ x 8½. 21851-1

THE PHILOSOPHY OF HISTORY, Georg W. Hegel. Great classic of Western thought develops concept that history is not chance but rational process, the evolution of freedom. 457pp. 5⅜ x 8½. 20112-0

THE BOOK OF TEA, Kakuzo Okakura. Minor classic of the Orient: entertaining, charming explanation, interpretation of traditional Japanese culture in terms of tea ceremony. 94pp. 5⅜ x 8½. 20070-1

LIFE IN ANCIENT EGYPT, Adolf Erman. Fullest, most thorough, detailed older account with much not in more recent books, domestic life, religion, magic, medicine, commerce, much more. Many illustrations reproduce tomb paintings, carvings, hieroglyphs, etc. 597pp. 5⅜ x 8½. 22632-8

SUNDIALS, Their Theory and Construction, Albert Waugh. Far and away the best, most thorough coverage of ideas, mathematics concerned, types, construction, adjusting anywhere. Simple, nontechnical treatment allows even children to build several of these dials. Over 100 illustrations. 230pp. 5⅜ x 8½. 22947-5

THEORETICAL HYDRODYNAMICS, L. M. Milne-Thomson. Classic exposition of the mathematical theory of fluid motion, applicable to both hydrodynamics and aerodynamics. Over 600 exercises. 768pp. 6⅛ x 9¼. 68970-0

SONGS OF EXPERIENCE: Facsimile Reproduction with 26 Plates in Full Color, William Blake. 26 full-color plates from a rare 1826 edition. Includes "The Tyger," "London," "Holy Thursday," and other poems. Printed text of poems. 48pp. 5¼ x 7. 24636-1

OLD-TIME VIGNETTES IN FULL COLOR, Carol Belanger Grafton (ed.). Over 390 charming, often sentimental illustrations, selected from archives of Victorian graphics—pretty women posing, children playing, food, flowers, kittens and puppies, smiling cherubs, birds and butterflies, much more. All copyright-free. 48pp. 9¼ x 12¼. 27269-9

PERSPECTIVE FOR ARTISTS, Rex Vicat Cole. Depth, perspective of sky and sea, shadows, much more, not usually covered. 391 diagrams, 81 reproductions of drawings and paintings. 279pp. 5⅜ x 8½. 22487-2

DRAWING THE LIVING FIGURE, Joseph Sheppard. Innovative approach to artistic anatomy focuses on specifics of surface anatomy, rather than muscles and bones. Over 170 drawings of live models in front, back and side views, and in widely varying poses. Accompanying diagrams. 177 illustrations. Introduction. Index. 144pp. 8⅜ x11¼. 26723-7

GOTHIC AND OLD ENGLISH ALPHABETS: 100 Complete Fonts, Dan X. Solo. Add power, elegance to posters, signs, other graphics with 100 stunning copyright-free alphabets: Blackstone, Dolbey, Germania, 97 more–including many lower-case, numerals, punctuation marks. 104pp. 8⅛ x 11. 24695-7

HOW TO DO BEADWORK, Mary White. Fundamental book on craft from simple projects to five-bead chains and woven works. 106 illustrations. 142pp. 5⅜ x 8. 20697-1

THE BOOK OF WOOD CARVING, Charles Marshall Sayers. Finest book for beginners discusses fundamentals and offers 34 designs. "Absolutely first rate . . . well thought out and well executed."–E. J. Tangerman. 118pp. 7¾ x 10⅝. 23654-4

ILLUSTRATED CATALOG OF CIVIL WAR MILITARY GOODS: Union Army Weapons, Insignia, Uniform Accessories, and Other Equipment, Schuyler, Hartley, and Graham. Rare, profusely illustrated 1846 catalog includes Union Army uniform and dress regulations, arms and ammunition, coats, insignia, flags, swords, rifles, etc. 226 illustrations. 160pp. 9 x 12. 24939-5

WOMEN'S FASHIONS OF THE EARLY 1900s: An Unabridged Republication of "New York Fashions, 1909," National Cloak & Suit Co. Rare catalog of mail-order fashions documents women's and children's clothing styles shortly after the turn of the century. Captions offer full descriptions, prices. Invaluable resource for fashion, costume historians. Approximately 725 illustrations. 128pp. 8⅜ x 11¼. 27276-1

THE 1912 AND 1915 GUSTAV STICKLEY FURNITURE CATALOGS, Gustav Stickley. With over 200 detailed illustrations and descriptions, these two catalogs are essential reading and reference materials and identification guides for Stickley furniture. Captions cite materials, dimensions and prices. 112pp. 6½ x 9¼. 26676-1

EARLY AMERICAN LOCOMOTIVES, John H. White, Jr. Finest locomotive engravings from early 19th century: historical (1804–74), main-line (after 1870), special, foreign, etc. 147 plates. 142pp. 11⅜ x 8¼. 22772-3

THE TALL SHIPS OF TODAY IN PHOTOGRAPHS, Frank O. Braynard. Lavishly illustrated tribute to nearly 100 majestic contemporary sailing vessels: Amerigo Vespucci, Clearwater, Constitution, Eagle, Mayflower, Sea Cloud, Victory, many more. Authoritative captions provide statistics, background on each ship. 190 black-and-white photographs and illustrations. Introduction. 128pp. 8⅞ x 11¾. 27163-3

LITTLE BOOK OF EARLY AMERICAN CRAFTS AND TRADES, Peter Stockham (ed.). 1807 children's book explains crafts and trades: baker, hatter, cooper, potter, and many others. 23 copperplate illustrations. 140pp. 4⅝ x 6. 23336-7

VICTORIAN FASHIONS AND COSTUMES FROM HARPER'S BAZAR, 1867–1898, Stella Blum (ed.). Day costumes, evening wear, sports clothes, shoes, hats, other accessories in over 1,000 detailed engravings. 320pp. 9⅜ x 12¼. 22990-4

GUSTAV STICKLEY, THE CRAFTSMAN, Mary Ann Smith. Superb study surveys broad scope of Stickley's achievement, especially in architecture. Design philosophy, rise and fall of the Craftsman empire, descriptions and floor plans for many Craftsman houses, more. 86 black-and-white halftones. 31 line illustrations. Introduction 208pp. 6½ x 9¼. 27210-9

THE LONG ISLAND RAIL ROAD IN EARLY PHOTOGRAPHS, Ron Ziel. Over 220 rare photos, informative text document origin (1844) and development of rail service on Long Island. Vintage views of early trains, locomotives, stations, passengers, crews, much more. Captions. 8⅞ x 11¾. 26301-0

VOYAGE OF THE LIBERDADE, Joshua Slocum. Great 19th-century mariner's thrilling, first-hand account of the wreck of his ship off South America, the 35-foot boat he built from the wreckage, and its remarkable voyage home. 128pp. 5⅜ x 8½. 40022-0

TEN BOOKS ON ARCHITECTURE, Vitruvius. The most important book ever written on architecture. Early Roman aesthetics, technology, classical orders, site selection, all other aspects. Morgan translation. 331pp. 5⅜ x 8½. 20645-9

THE HUMAN FIGURE IN MOTION, Eadweard Muybridge. More than 4,500 stopped-action photos, in action series, showing undraped men, women, children jumping, lying down, throwing, sitting, wrestling, carrying, etc. 390pp. 7⅞ x 10⅝. 20204-6 Clothbd.

TREES OF THE EASTERN AND CENTRAL UNITED STATES AND CANADA, William M. Harlow. Best one-volume guide to 140 trees. Full descriptions, woodlore, range, etc. Over 600 illustrations. Handy size. 288pp. 4½ x 6⅜. 20395-6

SONGS OF WESTERN BIRDS, Dr. Donald J. Borror. Complete song and call repertoire of 60 western species, including flycatchers, juncoes, cactus wrens, many more–includes fully illustrated booklet. Cassette and manual 99913-0

GROWING AND USING HERBS AND SPICES, Milo Miloradovich. Versatile handbook provides all the information needed for cultivation and use of all the herbs and spices available in North America. 4 illustrations. Index. Glossary. 236pp. 5⅜ x 8½. 25058-X

BIG BOOK OF MAZES AND LABYRINTHS, Walter Shepherd. 50 mazes and labyrinths in all–classical, solid, ripple, and more–in one great volume. Perfect inexpensive puzzler for clever youngsters. Full solutions. 112pp. 8⅛ x 11. 22951-3

PIANO TUNING, J. Cree Fischer. Clearest, best book for beginner, amateur. Simple repairs, raising dropped notes, tuning by easy method of flattened fifths. No previous skills needed. 4 illustrations. 201pp. 5⅜ x 8½. 23267-0

HINTS TO SINGERS, Lillian Nordica. Selecting the right teacher, developing confidence, overcoming stage fright, and many other important skills receive thoughtful discussion in this indispensible guide, written by a world-famous diva of four decades' experience. 96pp. 5⅜ x 8½. 40094-8

THE COMPLETE NONSENSE OF EDWARD LEAR, Edward Lear. All nonsense limericks, zany alphabets, Owl and Pussycat, songs, nonsense botany, etc., illustrated by Lear. Total of 320pp. 5⅜ x 8½. (Available in U.S. only.) 20167-8

VICTORIAN PARLOUR POETRY: An Annotated Anthology, Michael R. Turner. 117 gems by Longfellow, Tennyson, Browning, many lesser-known poets. "The Village Blacksmith," "Curfew Must Not Ring Tonight," "Only a Baby Small," dozens more, often difficult to find elsewhere. Index of poets, titles, first lines. xxiii + 325pp. 5⅝ x 8¼. 27044-0

DUBLINERS, James Joyce. Fifteen stories offer vivid, tightly focused observations of the lives of Dublin's poorer classes. At least one, "The Dead," is considered a masterpiece. Reprinted complete and unabridged from standard edition. 160pp. 5$\frac{3}{16}$ x 8¼. 26870-5

GREAT WEIRD TALES: 14 Stories by Lovecraft, Blackwood, Machen and Others, S. T. Joshi (ed.). 14 spellbinding tales, including "The Sin Eater," by Fiona McLeod, "The Eye Above the Mantel," by Frank Belknap Long, as well as renowned works by R. H. Barlow, Lord Dunsany, Arthur Machen, W. C. Morrow and eight other masters of the genre. 256pp. 5⅜ x 8½. (Available in U.S. only.) 40436-6

THE BOOK OF THE SACRED MAGIC OF ABRAMELIN THE MAGE, translated by S. MacGregor Mathers. Medieval manuscript of ceremonial magic. Basic document in Aleister Crowley, Golden Dawn groups. 268pp. 5⅜ x 8½. 23211-5

NEW RUSSIAN-ENGLISH AND ENGLISH-RUSSIAN DICTIONARY, M. A. O'Brien. This is a remarkably handy Russian dictionary, containing a surprising amount of information, including over 70,000 entries. 366pp. 4½ x 6⅛. 20208-9

HISTORIC HOMES OF THE AMERICAN PRESIDENTS, Second, Revised Edition, Irvin Haas. A traveler's guide to American Presidential homes, most open to the public, depicting and describing homes occupied by every American President from George Washington to George Bush. With visiting hours, admission charges, travel routes. 175 photographs. Index. 160pp. 8¼ x 11. 26751-2

NEW YORK IN THE FORTIES, Andreas Feininger. 162 brilliant photographs by the well-known photographer, formerly with *Life* magazine. Commuters, shoppers, Times Square at night, much else from city at its peak. Captions by John von Hartz. 181pp. 9¼ x 10¾. 23585-8

INDIAN SIGN LANGUAGE, William Tomkins. Over 525 signs developed by Sioux and other tribes. Written instructions and diagrams. Also 290 pictographs. 111pp. 6⅛ x 9¼. 22029-X

CATALOG OF DOVER BOOKS

ANATOMY: A Complete Guide for Artists, Joseph Sheppard. A master of figure drawing shows artists how to render human anatomy convincingly. Over 460 illustrations. 224pp. 8⅜ x 11¼. 27279-6

MEDIEVAL CALLIGRAPHY: Its History and Technique, Marc Drogin. Spirited history, comprehensive instruction manual covers 13 styles (ca. 4th century through 15th). Excellent photographs; directions for duplicating medieval techniques with modern tools. 224pp. 8⅜ x 11¼. 26142-5

DRIED FLOWERS: How to Prepare Them, Sarah Whitlock and Martha Rankin. Complete instructions on how to use silica gel, meal and borax, perlite aggregate, sand and borax, glycerine and water to create attractive permanent flower arrangements. 12 illustrations. 32pp. 5⅜ x 8½. 21802-3

EASY-TO-MAKE BIRD FEEDERS FOR WOODWORKERS, Scott D. Campbell. Detailed, simple-to-use guide for designing, constructing, caring for and using feeders. Text, illustrations for 12 classic and contemporary designs. 96pp. 5⅜ x 8½. 25847-5

SCOTTISH WONDER TALES FROM MYTH AND LEGEND, Donald A. Mackenzie. 16 lively tales tell of giants rumbling down mountainsides, of a magic wand that turns stone pillars into warriors, of gods and goddesses, evil hags, powerful forces and more. 240pp. 5⅜ x 8½. 29677-6

THE HISTORY OF UNDERCLOTHES, C. Willett Cunnington and Phyllis Cunnington. Fascinating, well-documented survey covering six centuries of English undergarments, enhanced with over 100 illustrations: 12th-century laced-up bodice, footed long drawers (1795), 19th-century bustles, 19th-century corsets for men, Victorian "bust improvers," much more. 272pp. 5⅝ x 8¼. 27124-2

ARTS AND CRAFTS FURNITURE: The Complete Brooks Catalog of 1912, Brooks Manufacturing Co. Photos and detailed descriptions of more than 150 now very collectible furniture designs from the Arts and Crafts movement depict davenports, settees, buffets, desks, tables, chairs, bedsteads, dressers and more, all built of solid, quarter-sawed oak. Invaluable for students and enthusiasts of antiques, Americana and the decorative arts. 80pp. 6½ x 9¼. 27471-3

WILBUR AND ORVILLE: A Biography of the Wright Brothers, Fred Howard. Definitive, crisply written study tells the full story of the brothers' lives and work. A vividly written biography, unparalleled in scope and color, that also captures the spirit of an extraordinary era. 560pp. 6⅛ x 9¼. 40297-5

THE ARTS OF THE SAILOR: Knotting, Splicing and Ropework, Hervey Garrett Smith. Indispensable shipboard reference covers tools, basic knots and useful hitches; handsewing and canvas work, more. Over 100 illustrations. Delightful reading for sea lovers. 256pp. 5⅜ x 8½. 26440-8

FRANK LLOYD WRIGHT'S FALLINGWATER: The House and Its History, Second, Revised Edition, Donald Hoffmann. A total revision–both in text and illustrations–of the standard document on Fallingwater, the boldest, most personal architectural statement of Wright's mature years, updated with valuable new material from the recently opened Frank Lloyd Wright Archives. "Fascinating"–*The New York Times.* 116 illustrations. 128pp. 9¼ x 10¾. 27430-6

PHOTOGRAPHIC SKETCHBOOK OF THE CIVIL WAR, Alexander Gardner. 100 photos taken on field during the Civil War. Famous shots of Manassas Harper's Ferry, Lincoln, Richmond, slave pens, etc. 244pp. 10⅝ x 8¼. 22731-6

FIVE ACRES AND INDEPENDENCE, Maurice G. Kains. Great back-to-the-land classic explains basics of self-sufficient farming. The one book to get. 95 illustrations. 397pp. 5⅜ x 8½. 20974-1

SONGS OF EASTERN BIRDS, Dr. Donald J. Borror. Songs and calls of 60 species most common to eastern U.S.: warblers, woodpeckers, flycatchers, thrushes, larks, many more in high-quality recording. Cassette and manual 99912-2

A MODERN HERBAL, Margaret Grieve. Much the fullest, most exact, most useful compilation of herbal material. Gigantic alphabetical encyclopedia, from aconite to zedoary, gives botanical information, medical properties, folklore, economic uses, much else. Indispensable to serious reader. 161 illustrations. 888pp. 6½ x 9¼. 2-vol. set. (Available in U.S. only.) Vol. I: 22798-7
Vol. II: 22799-5

HIDDEN TREASURE MAZE BOOK, Dave Phillips. Solve 34 challenging mazes accompanied by heroic tales of adventure. Evil dragons, people-eating plants, blood-thirsty giants, many more dangerous adversaries lurk at every twist and turn. 34 mazes, stories, solutions. 48pp. 8¼ x 11. 24566-7

LETTERS OF W. A. MOZART, Wolfgang A. Mozart. Remarkable letters show bawdy wit, humor, imagination, musical insights, contemporary musical world; includes some letters from Leopold Mozart. 276pp. 5⅜ x 8½. 22859-2

BASIC PRINCIPLES OF CLASSICAL BALLET, Agrippina Vaganova. Great Russian theoretician, teacher explains methods for teaching classical ballet. 118 illustrations. 175pp. 5⅜ x 8½. 22036-2

THE JUMPING FROG, Mark Twain. Revenge edition. The original story of The Celebrated Jumping Frog of Calaveras County, a hapless French translation, and Twain's hilarious "retranslation" from the French. 12 illustrations. 66pp. 5⅜ x 8½. 22686-7

BEST REMEMBERED POEMS, Martin Gardner (ed.). The 126 poems in this superb collection of 19th- and 20th-century British and American verse range from Shelley's "To a Skylark" to the impassioned "Renascence" of Edna St. Vincent Millay and to Edward Lear's whimsical "The Owl and the Pussycat." 224pp. 5⅜ x 8½. 27165-X

COMPLETE SONNETS, William Shakespeare. Over 150 exquisite poems deal with love, friendship, the tyranny of time, beauty's evanescence, death and other themes in language of remarkable power, precision and beauty. Glossary of archaic terms. 80pp. 5$\frac{3}{16}$ x 8¼. 26686-9

THE BATTLES THAT CHANGED HISTORY, Fletcher Pratt. Eminent historian profiles 16 crucial conflicts, ancient to modern, that changed the course of civilization. 352pp. 5⅜ x 8½. 41129-X

THE WIT AND HUMOR OF OSCAR WILDE, Alvin Redman (ed.). More than 1,000 ripostes, paradoxes, wisecracks: Work is the curse of the drinking classes; I can resist everything except temptation; etc. 258pp. 5⅜ x 8½.   20602-5

SHAKESPEARE LEXICON AND QUOTATION DICTIONARY, Alexander Schmidt. Full definitions, locations, shades of meaning in every word in plays and poems. More than 50,000 exact quotations. 1,485pp. 6½ x 9¼. 2-vol. set.
Vol. 1: 22726-X
Vol. 2: 22727-8

SELECTED POEMS, Emily Dickinson. Over 100 best-known, best-loved poems by one of America's foremost poets, reprinted from authoritative early editions. No comparable edition at this price. Index of first lines. 64pp. 5³⁄₁₆ x 8¼.   26466-1

THE INSIDIOUS DR. FU-MANCHU, Sax Rohmer. The first of the popular mystery series introduces a pair of English detectives to their archnemesis, the diabolical Dr. Fu-Manchu. Flavorful atmosphere, fast-paced action, and colorful characters enliven this classic of the genre. 208pp. 5³⁄₁₆ x 8¼.   29898-1

THE MALLEUS MALEFICARUM OF KRAMER AND SPRENGER, translated by Montague Summers. Full text of most important witchhunter's "bible," used by both Catholics and Protestants. 278pp. 6⅝ x 10.   22802-9

SPANISH STORIES/CUENTOS ESPAÑOLES: A Dual-Language Book, Angel Flores (ed.). Unique format offers 13 great stories in Spanish by Cervantes, Borges, others. Faithful English translations on facing pages. 352pp. 5⅜ x 8½.   25399-6

GARDEN CITY, LONG ISLAND, IN EARLY PHOTOGRAPHS, 1869–1919, Mildred H. Smith. Handsome treasury of 118 vintage pictures, accompanied by carefully researched captions, document the Garden City Hotel fire (1899), the Vanderbilt Cup Race (1908), the first airmail flight departing from the Nassau Boulevard Aerodrome (1911), and much more. 96pp. 8⅞ x 11¾.   40669-5

OLD QUEENS, N.Y., IN EARLY PHOTOGRAPHS, Vincent F. Seyfried and William Asadorian. Over 160 rare photographs of Maspeth, Jamaica, Jackson Heights, and other areas. Vintage views of DeWitt Clinton mansion, 1939 World's Fair and more. Captions. 192pp. 8⅞ x 11.   26358-4

CAPTURED BY THE INDIANS: 15 Firsthand Accounts, 1750-1870, Frederick Drimmer. Astounding true historical accounts of grisly torture, bloody conflicts, relentless pursuits, miraculous escapes and more, by people who lived to tell the tale. 384pp. 5⅜ x 8½.   24901-8

THE WORLD'S GREAT SPEECHES (Fourth Enlarged Edition), Lewis Copeland, Lawrence W. Lamm, and Stephen J. McKenna. Nearly 300 speeches provide public speakers with a wealth of updated quotes and inspiration—from Pericles' funeral oration and William Jennings Bryan's "Cross of Gold Speech" to Malcolm X's powerful words on the Black Revolution and Earl of Spenser's tribute to his sister, Diana, Princess of Wales. 944pp. 5⅜ x 8⅜.   40903-1

THE BOOK OF THE SWORD, Sir Richard F. Burton. Great Victorian scholar/adventurer's eloquent, erudite history of the "queen of weapons"—from prehistory to early Roman Empire. Evolution and development of early swords, variations (sabre, broadsword, cutlass, scimitar, etc.), much more. 336pp. 6⅛ x 9¼.
25434-8

AUTOBIOGRAPHY: The Story of My Experiments with Truth, Mohandas K. Gandhi. Boyhood, legal studies, purification, the growth of the Satyagraha (nonviolent protest) movement. Critical, inspiring work of the man responsible for the freedom of India. 480pp. 5⅜ x 8½. (Available in U.S. only.) 24593-4

CELTIC MYTHS AND LEGENDS, T. W. Rolleston. Masterful retelling of Irish and Welsh stories and tales. Cuchulain, King Arthur, Deirdre, the Grail, many more. First paperback edition. 58 full-page illustrations. 512pp. 5⅜ x 8½. 26507-2

THE PRINCIPLES OF PSYCHOLOGY, William James. Famous long course complete, unabridged. Stream of thought, time perception, memory, experimental methods; great work decades ahead of its time. 94 figures. 1,391pp. 5⅜ x 8½. 2-vol. set.
Vol. I: 20381-6 Vol. II: 20382-4

THE WORLD AS WILL AND REPRESENTATION, Arthur Schopenhauer. Definitive English translation of Schopenhauer's life work, correcting more than 1,000 errors, omissions in earlier translations. Translated by E. F. J. Payne. Total of 1,269pp. 5⅜ x 8½. 2-vol. set. Vol. 1: 21761-2 Vol. 2: 21762-0

MAGIC AND MYSTERY IN TIBET, Madame Alexandra David-Neel. Experiences among lamas, magicians, sages, sorcerers, Bonpa wizards. A true psychic discovery. 32 illustrations. 321pp. 5⅜ x 8½. (Available in U.S. only.) 22682-4

THE EGYPTIAN BOOK OF THE DEAD, E. A. Wallis Budge. Complete reproduction of Ani's papyrus, finest ever found. Full hieroglyphic text, interlinear transliteration, word-for-word translation, smooth translation. 533pp. 6½ x 9¼. 21866-X

MATHEMATICS FOR THE NONMATHEMATICIAN, Morris Kline. Detailed, college-level treatment of mathematics in cultural and historical context, with numerous exercises. Recommended Reading Lists. Tables. Numerous figures. 641pp. 5⅜ x 8½. 24823-2

PROBABILISTIC METHODS IN THE THEORY OF STRUCTURES, Isaac Elishakoff. Well-written introduction covers the elements of the theory of probability from two or more random variables, the reliability of such multivariable structures, the theory of random function, Monte Carlo methods of treating problems incapable of exact solution, and more. Examples. 502pp. 5⅜ x 8½. 40691-1

THE RIME OF THE ANCIENT MARINER, Gustave Doré, S. T. Coleridge. Doré's finest work; 34 plates capture moods, subtleties of poem. Flawless full-size reproductions printed on facing pages with authoritative text of poem. "Beautiful. Simply beautiful."–*Publisher's Weekly*. 77pp. 9¼ x 12. 22305-1

NORTH AMERICAN INDIAN DESIGNS FOR ARTISTS AND CRAFTSPEOPLE, Eva Wilson. Over 360 authentic copyright-free designs adapted from Navajo blankets, Hopi pottery, Sioux buffalo hides, more. Geometrics, symbolic figures, plant and animal motifs, etc. 128pp. 8⅜ x 11. (Not for sale in the United Kingdom.) 25341-4

SCULPTURE: Principles and Practice, Louis Slobodkin. Step-by-step approach to clay, plaster, metals, stone; classical and modern. 253 drawings, photos. 255pp. 8⅛ x 11. 22960-2

THE INFLUENCE OF SEA POWER UPON HISTORY, 1660–1783, A. T. Mahan. Influential classic of naval history and tactics still used as text in war colleges. First paperback edition. 4 maps. 24 battle plans. 640pp. 5⅜ x 8½. 25509-3

CATALOG OF DOVER BOOKS

THE STORY OF THE TITANIC AS TOLD BY ITS SURVIVORS, Jack Winocour (ed.). What it was really like. Panic, despair, shocking inefficiency, and a little heroism. More thrilling than any fictional account. 26 illustrations. 320pp. 5⅜ x 8½.
20610-6

FAIRY AND FOLK TALES OF THE IRISH PEASANTRY, William Butler Yeats (ed.). Treasury of 64 tales from the twilight world of Celtic myth and legend: "The Soul Cages," "The Kildare Pooka," "King O'Toole and his Goose," many more. Introduction and Notes by W. B. Yeats. 352pp. 5⅜ x 8½.
26941-8

BUDDHIST MAHAYANA TEXTS, E. B. Cowell and others (eds.). Superb, accurate translations of basic documents in Mahayana Buddhism, highly important in history of religions. The Buddha-karita of Asvaghosha, Larger Sukhavativyuha, more. 448pp. 5⅜ x 8½.
25552-2

ONE TWO THREE . . . INFINITY: Facts and Speculations of Science, George Gamow. Great physicist's fascinating, readable overview of contemporary science: number theory, relativity, fourth dimension, entropy, genes, atomic structure, much more. 128 illustrations. Index. 352pp. 5⅜ x 8½.
25664-2

EXPERIMENTATION AND MEASUREMENT, W. J. Youden. Introductory manual explains laws of measurement in simple terms and offers tips for achieving accuracy and minimizing errors. Mathematics of measurement, use of instruments, experimenting with machines. 1994 edition. Foreword. Preface. Introduction. Epilogue. Selected Readings. Glossary. Index. Tables and figures. 128pp. 5⅜ x 8½.
40451-X

DALÍ ON MODERN ART: The Cuckolds of Antiquated Modern Art, Salvador Dalí. Influential painter skewers modern art and its practitioners. Outrageous evaluations of Picasso, Cézanne, Turner, more. 15 renderings of paintings discussed. 44 calligraphic decorations by Dalí. 96pp. 5⅜ x 8½. (Available in U.S. only.)
29220-7

ANTIQUE PLAYING CARDS: A Pictorial History, Henry René D'Allemagne. Over 900 elaborate, decorative images from rare playing cards (14th–20th centuries): Bacchus, death, dancing dogs, hunting scenes, royal coats of arms, players cheating, much more. 96pp. 9¼ x 12¼.
29265-7

MAKING FURNITURE MASTERPIECES: 30 Projects with Measured Drawings, Franklin H. Gottshall. Step-by-step instructions, illustrations for constructing handsome, useful pieces, among them a Sheraton desk, Chippendale chair, Spanish desk, Queen Anne table and a William and Mary dressing mirror. 224pp. 8⅛ x 11¼.
29338-6

THE FOSSIL BOOK: A Record of Prehistoric Life, Patricia V. Rich et al. Profusely illustrated definitive guide covers everything from single-celled organisms and dinosaurs to birds and mammals and the interplay between climate and man. Over 1,500 illustrations. 760pp. 7½ x 10⅛.
29371-8